The Mystery of God

The Mystery of God

compiled by Mrs. Írán Fúrútan Muhájir
Revised Edition 1979

BAHÁ'Í PUBLISHING TRUST
27 RUTLAND GATE LONDON SW7 1PD

Published by the Bahá'í Publishing Trust
27, Rutland Gate, London SW7 1PD

©Copyright 1971 Mrs. Írán Fúrútan Muhájir
Revised edition 1979

First published by the Bahá'í Publishing Trust
of India in commemoration of the fiftieth
anniversary of the passing of 'Abdu'l-Bahá

ISBN 0 900125 44 6

Printed and bound in Great Britain by
Morrison & Gibb Ltd, London and Edinburgh

"O 'Abdu'l-Bahá"
Persian calligraphy by Mishkin-Qalam

ای امتِ ملکوت ترا افروختن نموده و نمایم در هر دم ملکوتِ بهجت فزایم و! تهلّل کنم ،! در هر روزی روحی تازه یابی و قوّتی روحانی جوئی وسببِ روشنائی عالم انسانی شوی شمع پر نوری گردی و مشهور بر تقوی شوی سببِ مرحمتِ نفوس شوی و بنا دی ملکوت الله کردی و ستارۀ روشن شوی ممتثل و مسئلتن و ارد کشیده نهایتِ محبت و مهربانی! از دیده و این نامۀ را بجلوۀ خویش میگذارم ،! از فرا اتش جنان بر افروزی که در قلوب آتش محبت را شعله زند
ع ع

Facsimile of 'Abdu'l-Bahá's handwriting.

"*Remember, whether or not I be on earth, My presence will be with you always.*"
— '*Abdu'l-Bahá*

Contents

		Page
1	Him Whom God Hath Purposed	13
2	The Most Mighty Branch	14
3	Branch of Holiness	17
4	The Most Perfect Bounty	18
5	The Mainspring of the Oneness of Humanity	21
6	'Abdu'l-Bahá	22
7	The Centre of the Covenant	25
8	Bahá'u'lláh's Tablets Addressed to 'Abdu'l-Bahá	45
9	The Master	57
10	The Successor of the Manifestation of God	68
11	Tumultuous Years	75
12	Entombment of the Báb's Remains on Mt. Carmel	93
13	His Travels	115
14	Glimpses of His Talks and Writings	161
15	The War Years	215
16	The Passing of 'Abdu'l-Bahá	230
17	Significance of the Station of 'Abdu'l-Bahá	262
18	Extracts from the Will and Testament of 'Abdu'l-Bahá	271
19	The Greatest Holy Leaf	278
20	Passages from Tablets revealed by Bahá'u'lláh	289

		Page
21	Passages from Tablets revealed by 'Abdu'l-Bahá	293
22	The Purest Branch	305
23	Navváb	313
24	The Tablet of Visitation	321

Him Whom God Hath Purposed

WHEN the ocean of My presence hath ebbed and the Book of My Revelation is ended, turn your faces toward Him Whom God hath purposed, Who hath branched from this Ancient Root.

* * *

When the Mystic Dove will have winged its flight from its Sanctuary of Praise and sought its far-off goal, its hidden habitation, refer ye whatsoever ye understand not in the Book to Him Who hath branched from this mighty Stock.

—Bahá'u'lláh

The Most Mighty Branch

THE Will of the divine Testator is this: It is incumbent upon the Aghsán, the Afnán and My kindred to turn, one and all, their faces towards the Most Mighty Branch. Consider that which We have revealed in Our Most Holy Book: 'When the ocean of My presence hath ebbed and the Book of My Revelation is ended, turn your faces toward Him Whom God hath purposed, Who hath branched from this Ancient Root.' The object of this sacred Verse is none other except the Most Mighty Branch ('Abdu'l-Bahá).

Thus have We graciously revealed unto you our potent Will, and I am verily the Gracious, the All Powerful.

Branch of Holiness

THERE hath branched from the Sadratu'l-Muntahá this sacred and glorious Being, this Branch of Holiness; well is it with him that hath sought His shelter and abideth beneath His shadow. Verily the Limb of the Law of God hath sprung forth from this root which God Hath firmly implanted in the Ground of His Will, and Whose Branch hath been so uplifted as to encompass the whole of creation.

Magnified be He, therefore, for this sublime, this blessed, this mighty, this exalted Handiwork! . . . A Word hath, as a token of Our grace, gone forth from the Most Great Tablet—a Word which God hath adorned with the ornament of His own Self, and made it sovereign over the earth and all that is therein, and a sign of His greatness and power among its people.

The Most Perfect Bounty

RENDER thanks unto God, O people, for His appearance; for verily He is the most great Favour unto you, the most perfect bounty upon you; and through Him every mouldering bone is quickened. Whoso turneth towards Him hath turned towards God, and whoso turneth away from Him hath turned away from My Beauty, hath repudiated My Proof, and transgressed against Me. He is the Trust of God amongst you, His charge within you, His manifestation unto you and His appearance among His favoured servants . . . We have sent Him down in the form of a human temple. Blest and sanctified be God Who createth whatsoever He willeth through His inviolable, His infallible decree. They who deprive themselves of the Shadow of the Branch, are lost in the wilderness of error, are consumed by the heat of worldly desires, and are of those who will assuredly perish.

'Abdu'l-Bahá and Purest Branch with friends in Adrianople

The Mainspring of the Oneness of Humanity

HE is, and should for all time be regarded, first and foremost, as the Centre and Pivot of Bahá'u'lláh's peerless and all-enfolding Covenant, His most exalted handiwork, the stainless Mirror of His light, the perfect Exemplar of His teachings, the unerring Interpreter of His Word, the embodiment of every Bahá'í ideal, the incarnation of every Bahá'í virtue, the Most Mighty Branch sprung from the Ancient Root, the Limb of the Law of God, the Being *"round Whom all names revolve,"* the Mainspring of the Oneness of Humanity, the Ensign of the Most Great Peace, the Moon of the Central Orb of this most holy Dispensation—styles and titles that are implicit and find their truest, their highest and fairest expression in the magic name 'Abdu'l-Bahá. He is, above and beyond these appellations, the *"Mystery of God"* —an expression which Bahá'u'lláh Himself has chosen to designate Him, and which, while it does not by any means justify us to assign to Him the station of Prophethood, indicates how in the person of 'Abdu'l-Bahá the incompatible characteristics of a human nature and superhuman knowledge and perfection have been blended and are completely harmonized.

'Abdu'l-Bahá

BUT if any soul asks concerning the station of this Servant, the answer is —'Abdu'l-Bahá. If he inquires after the meaning of the Branch, the answer is—'Abdu'l-Bahá. If he desires to know the significance of the verse regarding The Branch, the answer is—'Abdu'l-Bahá. If he insists upon the explanation of the meaning of "The Branch extended from the Ancient Root", the answer is—'Abdu'l-Bahá.

* * *

My name is 'Abdu'l-Bahá. My qualification is 'Abdu'l-Bahá. My reality is 'Abdu'l-Bahá. My praise is 'Abdu'l-Bahá. Thraldom to the Blessed Perfection is my glorious and refulgent diadem, and servitude to all the human race my perpetual religion . . . No name, no title, no mention, no commendation have I, nor will ever have, except 'Abdu'l-Bahá. This is my longing. This is my greatest yearning. This is my eternal life. This is my everlasting glory.

The Centre of the Covenant

IN the Book of Aqdas, He has given positive command in two clear instances and has explicitly appointed the Interpreter of the Book. Also in all the Divine Tablets, especially in the Chapter of The Branch—all the meanings of which mean the Servitude of 'Abdu'l-Bahá, that is 'Abdu'l-Bahá—all that was needed to explain the Centre of the Covenant and the Interpreter of the Book has been revealed from the Supreme Pen. Now as 'Abdu'l-Bahá is the Interpreter of the Book He says that the "Chapter of The Branch" means 'Abdu'l-Bahá, that is, the Servitude of 'Abdu'l-Bahá, and none other.

IF a soul shall utter a word without the sanction of the Covenant, he is not firm. Bahá'u'lláh appointed a Covenant to ward off dissensions: so that no one can have his own opinion—so that the Centre can be referred to. There were dissensions in the time of Christ because there was no Centre. This is the reality of the question. Whatever the Centre of the Covenant says is correct. No one shall speak a word of himself. Bahá'u'lláh has called down the vengeance of God upon anyone who violates the Covenant. Beware! Beware! Lest ye be shaken: remain firm even if the people of heaven try to shake you. Firmness in the Covenant is not mere words. The command is explicit.

'Abdu'l-Bahá

Painting by Munsen

THAT which has come out of the Centre of the Covenant you must take fast hold of. That which issues from my lips and that which is written with my pen is the reality. With this you can irrigate the vineyard of God. With this you can make the tree of the Cause of God become verdant. Through this the name of the Kingdom of God will be spread over the world. Through this the sun of reality will shine. Through this the clouds of mercy will pour down.

BE ye assured with the greatest assurance that, verily, God will help those who are firm in His Covenant in every matter, through His confirmation and favour, the lights of which will shine forth unto the east of the earth, as well as the west thereof. He will make them the signs of guidance among the creation and as shining and glittering stars from all horizons.

'Abdu'l-Bahá in Haifa garden

'Abdu'l-Bahá leaving Pilgrim House

THE power of the Covenant is as the heat of the sun which quickeneth and promoteth the development of all created things on earth. The light of the Covenant, in like manner, is the educator of the minds, the spirits, the hearts and souls of men.

'Abdu'l-Bahá seated in gateway at No. 7 Haparsim Street

BUT in this Dispensation of the Blessed Beauty (Bahá'u'lláh) among its distinctions is that He did not leave people in perplexity. He entered into a Covenant and Testament with the people. He appointed a Centre of the Covenant. He wrote with His own pen and revealed it in the Kitáb-i-Aqdas, the Book of Laws, and Kitáb-i-'Ahd, the Book of the Covenant, appointing Him ('Abdu'l-Bahá) the Expounder of the Book. You must ask Him ('Abdu'l-Bahá) regarding the meanings of the texts of the verses. Whatsoever He says is correct. Outside of this, in numerous Tablets He (Bahá'u'lláh) has explicitly recorded it, with clear, sufficient, valid, and forceful statements. In the Tablet of the Branch He explicitly states: "Whatsoever The Branch says is right, or correct; and every person must obey The Branch with his life, with his heart, with his tongue. Without His will, not a word shall anyone utter." This is an explicit text of the Blessed Beauty. So there is no excuse left for anybody. No soul shall, of himself, speak anything. Whatsoever His ('Abdu'l-Bahá's) tongue utters, whatsoever His pen records, that is correct; according to the explicit text of Bahá'u'lláh in the Tablet of the Branch.

THE Blessed Beauty is the Sun of Truth, and His light the light of truth. The Báb is likewise the Sun of Truth, and His light the light of truth . . . My station is the station of servitude—a servitude which is complete, pure and real, firmly established, enduring, obvious, explicitly revealed and subject to no interpretation whatever . . . I am the Interpreter of the Word of God; such is my interpretation.

Bahá'u'lláh's Tablets Addressed to 'Abdu'l-Bahá

O Thou Who art the apple of Mine eye. My glory, the ocean of My loving-kindness, the sun of My bounty, the heaven of My mercy rest upon Thee. We pray God to illumine the world through Thy knowledge and wisdom, to ordain for Thee that which will gladden Thine heart and impart consolation to Thine eyes.

'Abdu'l-Bahá walking in Haifa

WE have made Thee a shelter for all mankind, a shield unto all who are in heaven and on earth, a stronghold for whosoever hath believed in God, the Incomparable, the All-Knowing. God grant that through Thee He may protect them, may enrich and sustain them, that He may inspire Thee with that which shall be a wellspring of wealth unto all created things, an ocean of bounty unto all men, and the dayspring of mercy unto all peoples.

THE glory of God rest upon Thee, and upon whosoever serveth Thee and circleth around Thee. Woe, great woe, betide him that opposeth and injureth Thee. Well is it with him that sweareth fealty to Thee; the fire of hell torment him who is Thine enemy.

THOU knowest, O my God, that I desire for Him naught except that which Thou didst desire, and have chosen Him for no purpose save that which Thou hadst intended for Him. Render Him victorious, therefore, through Thy hosts of earth and heaven . . . Ordain, I beseech Thee, by the ardour of My love for Thee and My yearning to manifest Thy Cause, for Him, as well as for them that love Him, that which Thou hast destined for thy Messengers and the Trustees of Thy Revelation. Verily, Thou art the Almighty, the All-powerful.

ALL the atoms of the earth have announced unto all created things that from behind the gate of the Prison-city there hath appeared and above its horizon there hath shone forth the Orb of the beauty of the great, the Most Mighty Branch of God—His ancient and immutable Mystery—proceeding on its way to another land. Sorrow, thereby, hath enveloped this Prison-city, whilst another land rejoiceth . . . Blessed, doubly blessed, is the ground which His footsteps have trodden, the eye that hath been cheered by the beauty of His countenance, the ear that hath been honoured by hearkening to His call, the heart that hath tasted the sweetness of His love, the breast that hath dilated through His remembrance, the pen that hath voiced His praise, the scroll that hath borne the testimony of His writings.

'Abdu'l-Bahá in garden at No. 7 Haparsim Street

'Abdu'l-Bahá at Bahjí

'Abdu'l-Bahá in front yard of Haifa house

The Master

HE it was Whose auspicious birth occurred on that never-to-be-forgotten night when the Báb laid bare the transcendental character of His Mission to His first disciple Mullá Ḥusayn. He it was Who, as a mere child, seated on the lap of Ṭáhirih, had registered the thrilling significance of the stirring challenge which that indomitable heroine had addressed to her fellow-disciple, the erudite and far-famed Vaḥíd. He it was Whose tender soul had been seared with the ineffaceable vision of a Father, haggard, dishevelled, freighted with chains, on the occasion of a visit, as a boy of nine, to the Síyáh-Chál of Ṭihrán. Against Him, in His early childhood, whilst His Father lay a prisoner in that dungeon, had been directed the malice of a mob of street urchins who pelted Him with stones, vilified Him and overwhelmed Him with ridicule. His had been the lot to share with His Father, soon after His release from imprisonment, the rigours and miseries of a cruel banishment from His native land, and the trials which culminated in His enforced withdrawal to the mountains of Kurdistán. He it was Who, in His inconsolable grief at His separation from an adored Father, had confided to Nabíl, as attested by him in his narrative, that He felt Himself to have grown old though still but a child of tender years. His had been the unique distinction of recognizing, while still in His childhood, the full glory of His Father's as yet unrevealed station, a recognition which had impelled Him to throw Himself at His feet and to spontaneously implore the privilege of laying down His life for His sake. From His pen, while still in His adolescence in Baghdád, had issued that superb commentary on a well-known Muḥammadan tradition, written at the suggestion of Bahá'u'lláh, in answer to a request made by 'Ali-Shawkat Páshá, which was so illuminating as to excite the unbounded admiration of its recipient. It was His discussions and discourses with the learned doctors with whom He came in contact in Baghdád that first aroused that general admiration for Him and for His knowledge which was steadily to increase as the circle of His acquaintances was widened, at a later date, first in Adrianople and then in 'Akká. It was to Him that the highly accomplished Khurshíd Páshá, the governor of Adrianople, had been moved to pay a public and glowing tribute when, in the presence of a number of distinguished divines of that city, his youthful Guest had, briefly and amazingly, resolved the intricacies of a problem that had baffled the minds of the assembled company— an achievement that affected so deeply the Páshá that from that time onwards he could hardly reconcile himself to that Youth's absence from such gatherings.

On Him Bahá'u'lláh, as the scope and influence of His Mission extended, had been led to

'Abdu'l-Bahá

'Abdu'l-Bahá riding up Mount Carmel

place an ever greater degree of reliance, by appointing Him, on numerous occasions, as His deputy, by enabling Him to plead His Cause before the public, by assigning Him the task of transcribing His Tablets, by allowing Him to assume the responsibility of shielding Him from His enemies, and by investing Him with the function of watching over and promoting the interests of His fellow-exiles and companions. He it was Who had been commissioned to undertake, as soon as circumstances might permit, the delicate and all-important task of purchasing the site that was to serve as the permanent resting-place of the Báb, of insuring the safe transfer of His remains to the Holy Land, and of erecting for Him a befitting sepulchre on Mt. Carmel. He it was Who had been chiefly instrumental in providing the necessary means for Bahá'u'lláh's release from His nine-year confinement within the city walls of 'Akká, and in enabling Him to enjoy, in the evening of His life, a measure of that peace and security from which He had so long been debarred. It was through His unremitting efforts that the illustrious Badí' had been granted his memorable interviews with Bahá'u'lláh, that the hostility evinced by several governors of 'Akká towards the exiled community had been transmuted into esteem and admiration, that the purchase of properties adjoining the Sea of Galilee and the River Jordan had been effected, and that the ablest and most valuable presentation of the early history of the Faith and of its tenets had been

'Abdu'l-Bahá at Bahjí

transmitted to posterity. It was through the extraordinarily warm reception accorded Him during His visit to Beirut, through His contact with Midḥat Páshá, a former Grand Vizir of Turkey, through his friendship with 'Azíz Páshá, whom He had previously known in Adrianople, and who had subsequently been promoted to the rank of Valí, and through His constant association with officials, notables and leading ecclesiastics who, in increasing number, had besought His presence, during the final years of His Father's ministry, that He had succeeded in raising the prestige of the Cause He had championed to a level it had never previously attained.

He alone had been accorded the privilege of being called "the Master", an honour from which His Father had strictly excluded all His other sons. Upon Him that loving and unerring Father had chosen to confer the unique title of "*Sirru'lláh*" (the Mystery of God), a designation so appropriate to One Who, though essentially human and holding a station radically and fundamentally different from that occupied by Bahá'u'lláh and His Forerunner, could still claim to be the perfect Exemplar of His Faith, to be endowed with superhuman knowledge, and to be regarded as the stainless mirror reflecting His light.

'Abdu'l-Bahá walking into No. 7 Haparsim Street

'*Abdu'l-Bahá with friends on Mount Carmel*

The Successor of the Manifestation of God

AND now to crown the inestimable honours, privileges and benefits showered upon Him, in ever increasing abundance, throughout the forty years of His Father's ministry in Ba<u>gh</u>dád, in Adrianople and in 'Akká, He had been elevated to the high office of Centre of Bahá'u'lláh's Covenant, and been made the successor of the Manifestation of God Himself—a position that was to empower Him to impart an extraordinary impetus to the international expansion of His Father's Faith, to amplify its doctrine, to beat down every barrier that would obstruct its march, and to call into being, and delineate the features of, its Administrative Order, the Child of the Covenant, and the Harbinger of that World Order whose establishment must needs signalize the advent of the Golden Age of the Bahá'í Dispensation.

'Abdu'l-Bahá's tent

HIS Cause, precious beyond the dreams and hopes of men; enshrining within its shell that pearl of great price to which the world, since its foundation, had been looking forward; confronted with colossal tasks of unimaginable complexity and urgency, was beyond a peradventure in safe keeping. His own beloved Son, the apple of His eye, His vicegerent on earth, the Executive of His authority, the Pivot of His Covenant, the Shepherd of His flock, the Exemplar of His faith, the Image of His perfections, the Mystery of His Revelation, the Interpreter of His mind, the Architect of His World Order, the Ensign of His Most Great Peace, the Focal Point of His unerring guidance—in a word, the occupant of an office without peer or equal in the entire field of religious history—stood guard over it, alert, fearless and determined to enlarge its limits, blazon abroad its fame, champion its interests and consummate its purpose.

The stirring proclamation 'Abdu'l-Bahá had penned, addressed to the rank and file of the followers of His Father, on the morrow of His ascension, as well as the prophecies He Himself had uttered in His Tablets, breathed a resolve and a confidence which the fruits garnered and the triumphs achieved in the course of a thirty-year ministry have abundantly justified.

'Abdu'l-Bahá with friends on Mount Carmel

'Abdu'l-Bahá in Howard McNutt's garden

AN orphan community had recognized in 'Abdu'l-Bahá, in its hour of desperate need, its Solace, its Guide, its Mainstay and Champion. The Light that had glowed with such dazzling brightness in the heart of Asia, and had, in the lifetime of Bahá'u'lláh, spread to the Near East, and illuminated the fringes of both the European and African continents, was to travel, through the impelling influence of the newly proclaimed Covenant, and almost immediately after the death of its Author, as far West as the North American continent, and from thence diffuse itself to the countries of Europe, and subsequently shed its radiance over both the Far East and Australasia.

Tumultuous Years

IT was in 1901, on the fifth day of the month of Jamádíyu'l-Avval 1319 A.H. (August 20) that 'Abdu'l-Bahá, upon His return from Bahjí where He had participated in the celebration of the anniversary of the Báb's Declaration, was informed, in the course of an interview with the governor of 'Akká, of Sulṭán 'Abdu'l-Hamíd's instructions ordering that the restrictions which had been gradually relaxed should be reimposed, and that He and His brothers should be strictly confined within the walls of that city. The Sulṭán's edict was at first rigidly enforced, the freedom of the exiled community was severely curtailed, while 'Abdu'l-Bahá had to submit, alone and unaided, to the prolonged interrogation of judges and officials, who required His presence for several consecutive days at government headquarters for the purpose of their investigations. One of His first acts was to intercede on behalf of His brothers, who had been peremptorily summoned and informed by the governor of the orders of the sovereign, an act which failed to soften their hostility or lessen their malevolent activities. Subsequently, through His intervention with the civil and military authorities, He succeeded in obtaining the freedom of His followers who resided in 'Akká, and in enabling them to continue to earn, without interference, the means of livelihood.

*   *   *

The gravity of the situation confronting 'Abdu'l-Bahá; the rumours that were being set afloat by a population that anticipated the gravest developments; the hints and allusions to the dangers threatening Him contained in newspapers published in Egypt and Syria; the aggressive attitude which His enemies increasingly assumed; the provocative behaviour of some of the inhabitants of 'Akká and Haifa who had been emboldened by the predictions and fabrications of these enemies regarding the fate awaiting a suspected community and its Leader, led Him to reduce the number of pilgrims, and even to suspend, for a time, their visits, and to issue special instructions that His mail be handled through an agent in Egypt rather than in Haifa; for a time He ordered that it should be held there pending further advice from Him. He, moreover, directed the believers, as well as His own secretaries, to collect and remove to a place of safety all the Bahá'í writings in their possession, and, urging them to transfer their residence to Egypt, went so far as to forbid their gathering, as was their wont, in His house. Even His numerous friends and admirers refrained, during the most turbulent days of this period, from calling upon Him, for fear of being implicated and of incurring the suspicion of the authorities. On certain days and nights, when the outlook was

'Abdu'l-Bahá in California

'Abdu'l-Bahá in America

at its darkest, the house in which He was living, and which had for many years been a focus of activity, was completely deserted. Spies, secretly and openly, kept watch around it, observing His every movement and restricting the freedom of His family.

The construction of the Báb's sepulchre, whose foundation-stone had been laid by Him on the site blessed and selected by Bahá'u'lláh, He, however, refused to suspend, or even interrupt, for however brief a period. Nor would He allow any obstacle, however formidable, to interfere with the daily flow of Tablets which poured forth, with prodigious rapidity and ever increasing volume, from His indefatigable pen, in answer to the vast number of letters, reports, inquiries, prayers, confessions of faith, apologies and eulogies received from countless followers and admirers in both the East and the West. Eye-witnesses have testified that, during that agitated and perilous period of His life, they had known Him to pen, with His own Hand, no less than ninety Tablets in a single day, and to pass many a night, from dusk to dawn, alone in His bed-chamber engaged in a correspondence which the pressure of His manifold responsibilities had prevented Him from attending to in the day-time.

It was during these troublous times, the most dramatic period of His ministry, when, in the hey-day of His life and in the full tide of His power, He, with inexhaustible energy, marvellous serenity and unshakable confidence, initiated and resistlessly prosecuted the varied enterprises associated with that ministry. It was during these times that the plan of the first Mashriqu'l-Adhkár of the Bahá'í world was conceived by Him, and its construction undertaken by His followers in the city of 'Ishqábád in Turkistán. It was during these times, despite the disturbances that agitated His native country, that instructions were issued by Him for the restoration of the holy and historic House of the Báb in Shíráz. It was during these times that the initial measures, chiefly through His constant encouragement, were taken which paved the way for the laying of the dedication stone, which He, in later years, placed with His own hands when visiting the site of the Mother Temple of the West on the shore of Lake Michigan. It was at this juncture that that celebrated compilation of His table talks, published under the title "Some Answered Questions", was made, talks given during the brief time He was able to spare, in the course of which certain fundamental aspects of His Father's Faith were elucidated, traditional and rational proofs of its validity adduced, and a great variety of subjects regarding the Christian Dispensation, the Prophets of God, Biblical prophecies, the origin and condition of man and other kindred themes authoritatively explained.

It was during the darkest hours of this period that, in a communication addressed to the Báb's cousin, the venerable Hájí Mírzá Muḥammad-Taqí, the chief builder of the Temple of 'Ishqábád, 'Abdu'l-Bahá, in stirring terms, proclaimed the immeasurable greatness of the Revelation of

Bahá'u'lláh, sounded the warnings foreshadowing the turmoil which its enemies, both far and near, would let loose upon the world, and prophesied in moving language, the ascendancy which the torchbearers of the Covenant would ultimately achieve over them. It was at an hour of grave suspense, during that same period, that He penned His Will and Testament, that immortal Document wherein He delineated the features of the Administrative Order which would arise after His passing, and would herald the establishment of that World Order, the advent of which the Báb had announced, and the laws and principles of which Bahá'u'lláh had already formulated. It was in the course of these tumultuous years that, through the instrumentality of the heralds and champions of a firmly instituted Covenant, He reared the embryonic institutions, administrative, spiritual, and educational, of a steadily expanding Faith in Persia, the cradle of that Faith, in the Great Republic of the West, the cradle of its Administrative Order, in the Dominion of Canada, in France, in England, in Germany, in Egypt, in 'Iráq, in Russia, in India, in Burma, in Japan, and even in the remote Pacific Islands. It was during these stirring times that a tremendous impetus was lent by Him to the translation, the publication and dissemination of Bahá'í literature, whose scope now included a variety of books and treatises, written in the Persian, the Arabic, the English, the Turkish, the French, the German, the Russian and Burmese languages. At His table, in those days, whenever there was a

lull in the storm raging about Him, there would gather pilgrims, friends and inquirers from most of the afore-mentioned countries, representative of the Christian, the Muslim, the Jewish, the Zoroastrian, the Hindu and Buddhist Faiths. To the needy thronging His doors and filling the courtyard of His house every Friday morning, in spite of the perils that environed Him, He would distribute alms with His own hands, with a regularity and generosity that won Him the title of "Father of the Poor". Nothing in those tempestuous days could shake His confidence, nothing would be allowed to interfere with His ministrations to the destitute, the orphan, the sick, and the down-trodden, nothing could prevent Him from calling in person upon those who were either incapacitated, or ashamed to solicit His aid. Adamant in His determination to follow the example of both the Báb and Bahá'u'lláh, nothing would induce Him to flee from His enemies, or escape from imprisonment, neither the advice tendered Him by the leading members of the exiled community in 'Akká, nor the insistent pleas of the Spanish Consul—a kinsman of the agent of an Italian steamship company—who, in his love for 'Abdu'l-Bahá and his anxiety to avert the threatening danger, had gone so far as to place at His disposal an Italian freighter, ready to provide Him a safe passage to any foreign port He might name.

So imperturbable was 'Abdu'l-Bahá's equanimity that, while rumours were being bruited about that He might be cast into the sea, or exiled to Fízán in Tripolitania, or hanged on the gallows, He, to the amazement of His friends and the amusement of His enemies, was to be seen planting trees and vines in the garden of His house, whose fruits, when the storm had blown over, He would bid His faithful gardener, Ismá'íl Áqá, pluck and present to those same friends and enemies on the occasion of their visits to Him.

... It was suddenly observed, one day at about sunset, that the ship, which had been lying off Haifa, had weighed anchor, and was heading towards 'Akká. The news spread rapidly among an excited population that the members of the Commission had embarked upon it. It was anticipated that it would stop long enough at 'Akká to take 'Abdu'l-Bahá on board, and then proceed to its destination. Consternation and anguish seized the members of His family when informed of the approach of the ship. The few believers who were left wept with grief at their impending separation from their Master. 'Abdu'l-Bahá could be seen, at that tragic hour, pacing, alone and silent, the courtyard of His house.

As dusk fell, however, it was suddenly noticed that the lights of the ship had swung round, and the vessel had changed her course. It now became evident that she was sailing direct for Constantinople. The intelligence was instantly communicated to 'Abdu'l-Bahá, Who, in the gathering darkness, was still pacing His courtyard. Some of the believers who had posted themselves at different points to watch the progress of the

'Abdu'l-Bahá in garden at No. 7 Haparsim Street

'Abdu'l-Bahá riding on donkey up Mount Carmel

ship hurried to confirm the joyful tidings. One of the direst perils that had ever threatened 'Abdu'l-Bahá's precious life was on that historic day, suddenly, providentially, and definitely averted.

Soon after the precipitate and wholly unexpected sailing of that ship news was received that a bomb had exploded in the path of the Sultán while he was returning to his palace from the mosque where he had been offering his Friday prayers.

A few days after this attempt on his life the Commission submitted its report to him; but he and his government were too preoccupied to consider the matter. The case was laid aside, and when, some months later, it was again brought forward it was abruptly closed forever by an event which, once and for all, placed the Prisoner of 'Akká beyond the power of His royal enemy. The "Young Turk" Revolution, breaking out swiftly and decisively in 1908, forced a reluctant despot to promulgate the constitution which he had suspended, and to release all religious and political prisoners held under the old régime. Even then a telegram had to be sent to Constantinople to inquire specifically whether 'Abdu'l-Bahá was included in the category of these prisoners, to which an affirmative reply was promptly received.

'Abdu'l-Bahá in garden at No. 7 Haparsim Street

Entombment of the Báb's Remains on Mt. Carmel

ABDU'L-BAHÁ'S unexpected and dramatic release from His forty-year confinement dealt a blow to the ambitions cherished by the Covenant-breakers as devastating as that which, a decade before, had shattered their hopes of undermining His authority and of ousting Him from His God-given position. Now, on the very morrow of His triumphant liberation a third blow befell them as stunning as those which preceded it and hardly less spectacular than they. Within a few months of the historic decree which set Him free, in the very year that witnessed the downfall of Sulṭán 'Abdu'l-Hamíd, that same power from on high which had enabled 'Abdu'l-Bahá to preserve inviolate the rights divinely conferred on Him, to establish His Father's Faith in the North American continent, and to triumph over His royal oppressor, enabled Him to achieve one of the most signal acts of His ministry: the removal of the Báb's remains from their place of concealment in Ṭihrán to Mt. Carmel. He Himself testified, on more than one occasion, that the safe transfer of these remains, the construction of a befitting mausoleum to receive them, and their final interment with His own hands in their permanent resting-place constituted one of the three principal objectives which, ever since the inception of His mission, He had conceived it His paramount duty to achieve. This act indeed deserves to rank as one of the outstanding events in the first Bahá'í century.

... the mangled bodies of the Báb and His fellow-martyr, Mírzá Muhammad-'Alí, were removed in the middle of the second night following their execution, through the pious intervention of Ḥájí Sulaymán Khán, from the edge of the moat where they had been cast to a silk factory owned by one of the believers of Mílán, and were laid the next day in a wooden casket, and thence carried to a place of safety. Subsequently, according to Bahá'u'lláh's instructions, they were transported to Ṭihrán and placed in the shrine of Imám-Zádih Ḥasan. They were later removed to the residence of Ḥájí Sulaymán Khán himself in the Sar-Chashmih quarter of the city, and from his house were taken to the shrine of Imám-Zádih Ma'ṣúm, where they remained concealed until the year 1284 A.H. (1867–1868), when a Tablet, revealed by Bahá'u'lláh in Adrianople, directed Mullá 'Ali-Akbar-i-Shahmírzádí and Jamál-i-Burújirdí to transfer them without delay to some other spot, an instruction which, in view of the subsequent reconstruction of that shrine, proved to have been providential.

Unable to find a suitable place in the suburb of Sháh 'Abdu'l 'Aẓím, Mullá 'Ali-Akbar and his companion continued their search until, on the road leading to Chashmih-'Alí, they came upon the abandoned and dilapidated Masjid-i-

'Abdu'l-Bahá at Stanford University, 8 October 1912

Mashá'u'lláh, where they deposited, within one of its walls, after dark, their precious burden, having first re-wrapt the remains in a silken shroud brought by them for that purpose. Finding, the next day to their consternation that the hiding-place had been discovered, they clandestinely carried the casket through the gate of the capital direct to the house of Mírzá Ḥasan-i-Vazír, a believer and son-in-law of Ḥájí Mírzá Siyyid 'Alíy-i-Tafríshí, the Majdu'l-Ashráf, where it remained for no less than fourteen months. The long-guarded secret of its whereabouts becoming known to the believers, they began to visit the house in such numbers that a communication had to be addressed by Mullá 'Alí-Akbar to Bahá'u'lláh, begging for guidance in the matter. Ḥájí Sháh Muḥammad-i-Manshádí, surnamed Amínu'l-Bayán, was accordingly commissioned to receive the Trust from him, and bidden to exercise the utmost secrecy as to its disposal.

Assisted by another believer, Ḥájí Sháh Muḥammad buried the casket beneath the floor of the inner sanctuary of the shrine of Imám-Zádih Zayd, where it lay undetected until Mírzá Asadu'lláh-i-Iṣfáhání was informed of its exact location through a chart forwarded to him by Bahá'u'lláh. Instructed by Bahá'u'lláh to conceal it elsewhere, he first removed the remains to his own house in Ṭihrán, after which they were deposited in several other localities such as the house of Ḥusayn-'Alíy-i-Isfáhání and that of Muḥammad-Karím-i-'Attár, where they remained hidden until the year 1316 (1899) A.H., when,

'Abdu'l-Bahá walking up to his room near the Shrine of the Báb

The Shrine of the Báb during 'Abdu'l-Bahá's lifetime

in pursuance of directions issued by 'Abdu'l-Bahá, this same Mírzá Asadu'lláh, together with a number of other believers, transported them by way of Iṣfáhán, Kirmánsháh, Baghdád and Damascus, to Beirut and thence by sea to 'Akká, arriving at their destination on the 19th of the month of Ramaḍán 1316 A.H. (January 31, 1899), fifty lunar years after the Báb's execution in Tabríz.

In the same year that this precious Trust reached the shores of the Holy Land and was delivered into the hands of 'Abdu'l-Bahá, He, ... drove to the recently purchased site which had been blessed and selected by Bahá'u'lláh on Mt. Carmel, and there laid, with His own hands, the foundation-stone of the edifice, the construction of which He, a few months later, was to commence. About that same time, the marble sarcophagus, designed to receive the body of the Báb, an offering of love from the Bahá'ís of Rangoon, had, at 'Abdu'l-Bahá's suggestion, been completed and shipped to Haifa.

No need to dwell on the manifold problems and preoccupations which, for almost a decade, continued to beset 'Abdu'l-Bahá until the victorious hour when He was able to bring to a final consummation the historic task entrusted to Him by His Father. The risks and perils with which Bahá'u'lláh and later His Son had been confronted in their efforts to insure, during half a century, the protection of those remains were but a prelude to the grave dangers which, at a later period, the Centre of the Covenant Himself had to

face in the course of the construction of the edifice designed to receive them, and indeed until the hour of His final release from His incarceration.

The long-drawnout negotiations with the shrewd and calculating owner of the building site of the holy Edifice, who, under the influence of the Covenant-breakers, refused for a long time to sell; the exorbitant price at first demanded for the opening of a road leading to that site and indispensable to the work of construction; the interminable objections raised by officials, high and low, whose easily aroused suspicions had to be allayed by repeated explanations and assurances given by 'Abdu'l-Bahá Himself; the dangerous situation created by the monstrous accusations brought by Mírzá Muhammad-'Alí and his associates regarding the character and purpose of that building; the delays and complications caused by 'Abdu'l-Bahá's prolonged and enforced absence from Haifa, and His consequent inability to supervise in person the vast undertaking He had initiated—all these were among the principal obstacles which He, at so critical a period in His ministry, had to face and surmount ere He could execute in its entirety the Plan, the outline of which Bahá'u'lláh had communicated to Him on the occasion of one of His visits to Mt. Carmel.

Painting of 'Abdu'l-Bahá by Sigismond Ivanowski

"EVERY stone of that building, every stone of the road leading to it," He many a time was heard to remark, "I have with infinite tears and at tremendous cost, raised and placed in position." "One night," He, according to an eye-witness, once observed, "I was so hemmed in by My anxieties that I had no other recourse than to recite and repeat over and over again a prayer of the Báb which I had in My possession, the recital of which greatly calmed Me. The next morning the owner of the plot himself came to Me, apologized and begged Me to purchase his property."

Finally, in the very year His royal adversary lost his throne, and at the time of the opening of the first American Bahá'í Convention, convened in Chicago for the purpose of creating a permanent national organization for the construction of the Mashriqu'l-Adhkár, 'Abdu'l-Bahá brought His undertaking to a successful conclusion, in spite of the incessant machinations of enemies both within and without. On the 28th of the month of Ṣafar 1327 A.H., the day of the first Naw-Rúz (1909), which He celebrated after His release from His confinement, 'Abdu'l-Bahá had the marble sarcophagus transported with great labour to the vault prepared for it, and in the evening,

by the light of a single lamp, He laid within it, with His own hands—in the presence of believers from the East and from the West and in circumstances at once solemn and moving—the wooden casket containing the sacred remains of the Báb and His companion.

When all was finished, and the earthly remains of the Martyr-Prophet of S͟híráz were, at long last, safely deposited for their everlasting rest in the bosom of God's holy mountain, 'Abdu'l-Bahá, Who had cast aside His turban, removed His shoes and thrown off His cloak, bent low over the still open sarcophagus, His silver hair waving about His head and His face transfigured and luminous, rested His forehead on the border of the wooden casket, and, sobbing aloud, wept with such a weeping that all those who were present wept with Him. That night He could not sleep, so overwhelmed was He with emotion.

"The most joyful tidings is this," He wrote later in a Tablet announcing to His followers the news of this glorious victory, "that the holy, the luminous body of the Báb . . . after having for sixty years been transferred from place to place, by reason of the ascendancy of the enemy, and from fear of the malevolent, and having known neither rest nor tranquillity has, through the mercy of the Abhá Beauty, been ceremoniously deposited, on the day of Naw-Rúz, within the sacred casket, in the exalted Shrine on Mt. Carmel . . . By a strange coincidence, on that same day of Naw-Rúz, a cablegram was received

'Abdu'l-Bahá in England

from Chicago, announcing that the believers in each of the American centres had elected a delegate and sent to that city . . . and definitely decided on the site and construction of the Mas͟hriqu'l-Ad͟hkár."

'Abdu'l-Bahá in garden surrounding the shrine of Bahá'u'lláh at Bahjí

His Travels

'ABDU'L-BAHÁ was at this time broken in health. He suffered from several maladies brought on by the strains and stresses of a tragic life spent almost wholly in exile and imprisonment. He was on the threshold of three-score years and ten. Yet as soon as He was released from His forty-year-long captivity, as soon as He had laid the Báb's body in a safe and permanent resting-place, and His mind was free of grievous anxieties connected with the execution of that priceless Trust, He arose with sublime courage, confidence and resolution to consecrate what little strength remained to Him, in the evening of His life, to a service of such heroic proportions that no parallel to it is to be found in the annals of the first Bahá'í century.

Indeed His three years of travel, first to Egypt, then to Europe and later to America, mark, if we would correctly appraise their historic importance, a turning point of the utmost significance in the history of the century. For the first time since the inception of the Faith, sixty-six years previously, its Head and supreme Representative burst asunder the shackles which had throughout the ministries of both the Báb and Bahá'u'lláh so grievously fettered its freedom. Though repressive measures still continued to circumscribe the activities of the vast majority of its adherents in the land of its birth, its recognized Leader was now vouchsafed a freedom of action which, with the exception of a brief interval in the course of the War of 1914–18, He was to continue to enjoy to the end of His life, and which has never since been withdrawn from its institutions at its world centre.

So momentous a change in the fortunes of the Faith was the signal for such an outburst of activity on His part as to dumbfound His followers in East and West with admiration and wonder, and exercise an imperishable influence on the course of its future history. He Who, in His own words, had entered prison as a youth and left it an old man, Who never in His life had faced a public audience, had attended no school, had never moved in Western circles, and was unfamiliar with Western customs and language, had arisen not only to proclaim from pulpit and platform, in some of the chief capitals of Europe and in the leading cities of the North American continent, the distinctive varieties enshrined in His Father's Faith, but to demonstrate as well the Divine origin of the Prophets gone before Him, and to disclose the nature of the tie binding them to that Faith.

Inflexibly resolved to undertake this arduous voyage, at whatever cost to His strength, at whatever risk to His life, He, quietly, and without any previous warning, on a September afternoon of the year 1910, the year following that which witnessed the downfall of Sulṭán 'Abdu'l-Ḥamíd

'Abdu'l-Bahá with children

and the formal entombment of the Báb's remains on Mt. Carmel, sailed for Egypt, sojourned for about a month in Port Said, and from thence embarked with the intention of proceeding to Europe, only to discover that the condition of His health necessitated His landing again at Alexandria and postponing His voyage. Fixing His residence in Ramleh, a suburb of Alexandria, and later visiting Zaytún and Cairo, He, on August 11 of the ensuing year, sailed with a party of four, on the S.S. Corsica for Marseilles and proceeded, after a brief stop at Thonon-les-Bains, to London, where He arrived on September 4, 1911. After a visit of about a month, He went to Paris, where He stayed for a period of nine weeks, returning to Egypt in December, 1911. Again taking up His residence in Ramleh, where He passed the winter, He embarked, on His second journey to the West, on the steamship Cedric, on March 25, 1912, sailing via Naples direct to New York where He arrived on April 11.

During these travels 'Abdu'l-Bahá displayed a vitality, a courage, a single-mindedness, a consecration to the task He had set Himself to achieve that excited the wonder and admiration of those who had the privilege of observing at close hand His daily acts. Indifferent to the sights and curiosities which habitually invite the attention of travellers and which the members of His entourage often wished Him to visit; careless alike of His comfort and His health; expending every ounce of His energy day after day from dawn till late at night; consistently refusing any gifts or

'Abdu'l-Bahá with large group in Germany

'Abdu'l-Bahá in Germany

'Abdu'l-Bahá with group in Stuttgart, Germany

contributions towards the expenses of His travels; unfailing in His solicitude for the sick, the sorrowful and the down-trodden; uncompromising in His championship of the underprivileged races and classes; bountiful as the rain in His generosity to the poor; contemptuous of the attacks launched against Him by vigilant and fanatical exponents of orthodoxy and sectarianism; marvellous in His frankness while demonstrating, from platform and pulpit, the prophetic Mission of Jesus Christ to the Jews, of the Divine origin of Islám in churches and synagogues, or the truth of Divine Revelation and the necessity of religion to materialists, atheists or agnostics; unequivocal in His glorification of Bahá'u'lláh at all times and within the sanctuaries of divers sects and denominations; adamant in His refusal, on several occasions, to curry the favour of people of title and wealth both in England and in the United States; and last but not least incomparable in the spontaneity, the genuineness and warmth of His sympathy and loving-kindness shown to friend and stranger alike, believer and unbeliever, rich and poor, high and low, whom He met, either intimately or casually, whether on board ship, or whilst pacing the streets, in parks or public squares, at receptions or banquets, in slums or mansions, in the gatherings of His followers or the assemblage of the learned, He, the incarnation of every Bahá'í virtue and the embodiment of every Bahá'í ideal, continued for three crowded years to trumpet to a world sunk in materialism and already in the shadow of war,

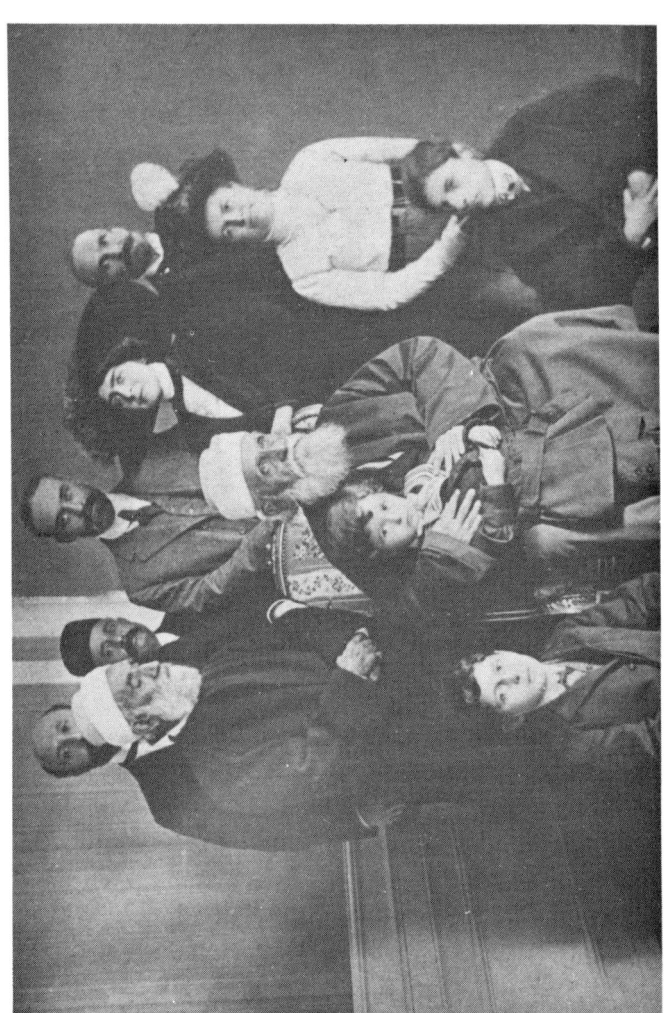

'Abdu'l-Bahá in Paris

'Abdu'l-Bahá in Paris

'Abdu'l-Bahá in England

the healing, the God-given truths enshrined in His Father's Revelation.

*   *   *

Whilst He sojourned in England the house placed at His disposal in Cadogan Gardens became a veritable mecca to all sorts and conditions of men, thronging to visit the Prisoner of 'Akká Who had chosen their great city as the first scene of His labours in the West. "O, these pilgrims, these guests, these visitors!" thus bears witness His devoted hostess during the time He spent in London, "Remembering those days, our ears are filled with the sound of their footsteps—as they came from every country in the world. Every day, all day long, a constant stream, an interminable procession! Ministers and missionaries, oriental scholars and occult students, practical men of affairs and mystics, Anglicans, Catholics, and Non-conformists, Theosophists and Hindus, Christian Scientists and doctors of medicine, Muslims, Buddhists and Zoroastrians. There also called: politicians, Salvation Army soldiers, and other workers for human good, women suffragists, journalists, writers, poets and healers, dressmakers and great ladies, artists and artisans, poor workless people and prosperous merchants, members of the dramatic and musical world, these all came; and none were too lowly, nor too great, to receive the sympathetic consideration of this holy Messenger, Who was ever giving His life for others' good."

'Abdu'l-Bahá in Paris, *1912*

*'Abdu'l-Bahá at the Clifton guest house, Bristol, England,
September 1911*

Meeting in the hall of Passmore Edwards Settlement, London.

"When 'Abdu'l-Bahá visited this country for the first time in 1912," a commentator on His American travels has written, "He found a large and sympathetic audience waiting to greet Him personally and to receive from His own lips His loving and spiritual message . . . Beyond the words spoken there was something indescribable in His personality that impressed profoundly all who came into His presence. The dome-like head, the patriarchal beard, the eyes that seemed to have looked beyond the reach of time and sense, the soft yet clearly penetrating voice, the translucent humility, the never failing love,—but above all, the sense of power mingled with gentleness that invested His whole being with a rare majesty of spiritual exaltation that both set Him apart, and yet that brought Him near to the lowliest soul,—it was all this, and much more that can never be defined, that have left with His many . . . friends, memories that are ineffaceable and unspeakably precious."

A survey, however inadequate of the varied and immense activities of 'Abdu'l-Bahá in His tour of Europe and America cannot leave without mention some of the strange incidents that would often accompany personal contact with Him. The bold determination of a certain indomitable youth who, fearing 'Abdu'l-Bahá would not be able to visit the Western states, and unable himself to pay for a train journey to New England, had travelled all the way from Minneapolis to Maine lying on the rods between the wheels of a train; the transformation effected in the life of

Taken on the eve of departure from Budapest to Vienna

'Abdu'l-Bahá with friends

the son of a country rector in England, who, in his misery and poverty, had resolved, whilst walking along the banks of the Thames, to put an end to his existence, and who, at the sight of 'Abdu'l-Bahá's photograph displayed in a shop window, had inquired about Him, hurried to His residence, and been so revived by His words of cheer and comfort as to abandon all thought of self-destruction; the extraordinary experience of a woman whose little girl, as the result of a dream she had had, insisted that Jesus Christ was in the world, and who, at the sight of 'Abdu'l-Bahá's picture exposed in the window of a magazine store, had instantly identified it as that of the Jesus Christ of her dream—an act which impelled her mother, after reading that 'Abdu'l-Bahá was in Paris, to take the next boat for Europe and hasten to attain His presence; the decision of the editor of a journal printed in Japan to break his journey to Tokyo at Constantinople, and travel to London for "the joy of spending one evening in His presence"; the touching scene when 'Abdu'l-Bahá, receiving from the hands of a Persian friend, recently arrived in London from 'Ishqábád, a cotton handkerchief containing a piece of dry black bread and a shrivelled apple—the offering of a poor Bahá'í workman in that city—opened it before His assembled guests, and, leaving His luncheon untouched, broke pieces off that bread, and partaking Himself of it shared it with those who were present—these are but a few of a host of incidents that shed a revealing light on some personal aspects of His memorable journeys.

'Abdu'l-Bahá walking near Lincoln Monument, Chicago, 1912

At home of Persian Consul-General, Topakyan, Morristown, New Jersey, 1912

Nor can certain scenes revolving around that majestic and patriarchal Figure, as He moved through the cities of Europe and America, be ever effaced from memory. The remarkable interview at which 'Abdu'l-Bahá, while placing lovingly His hand on the head of Archdeacon Wilberforce, answered his many questions, whilst that distinguished churchman sat on a low chair by His side; the still more remarkable scene when that same Archdeacon, after having knelt with his entire congregation to receive His benediction at St. John's the Divine, passed down the aisle to the vestry hand in hand with his Guest, whilst a hymn was being sung by the entire assembly standing; the sight of Jalálu'd-Dawlih, fallen prostrate at His feet, profuse in his apologies and imploring His forgiveness for his past iniquities; the enthusiastic reception accorded Him at Leland Stanford University when, before the gaze of well nigh two thousand professors and students, He discoursed on some of the noblest truths underlying His message to the West; the touching spectacle at Bowery Mission when four hundred of the poor of New York filed past Him, each receiving a piece of silver from His blessed hands; the acclamation of a Syrian woman in Boston who, pushing aside the crowd that had gathered around Him, flung herself at His feet, exclaiming, "I confess that in Thee I have recognized the Spirit of God and Jesus Christ Himself"; the no less fervent tribute paid Him by two admiring Arabs who, as He was leaving that city for Dublin, N.H., cast themselves before

Him, and, sobbing aloud, avowed that He was God's own Messenger to mankind; the vast congregation of two thousand Jews assembled in a synagogue in San Francisco, intently listening to His discourse as He demonstrated the validity of the claims advanced by both Jesus Christ and Muḥammad; the gathering He addressed one night in Montreal, at which, in the course of His speech, His turban fell from His head, so carried away was He by the theme He was expounding; the boisterous crowd in a very poor quarter of Paris, who, awed by His presence, reverently and silently made way for Him as He passed through their midst, while returning from a Mission Hall whose congregation He had been addressing; the characteristic gesture of a Zoroastrian physician who, arriving in breathless haste on the morning of 'Abdu'l-Bahá's departure from London to bid Him farewell, anointed with fragrant oil first His head and His breast, and then, touching the hands of all present, placed round His neck and shoulders a garland of rosebuds and lilies; the crowd of visitors arriving soon after dawn, patiently waiting on the doorsteps of His house in Cadogan Gardens until the door would be opened for their admittance; His majestic figure as He paced with a vigorous step the platform, or stood with hands upraised to pronounce the benediction, in church and synagogue alike, and before vast audiences of reverent listeners; the unsolicited mark of respect shown Him by distinguished society women in London, who would spontaneously curtsy when ushered

In Lincoln Park, Chicago, May 1912

'Abdu'l-Bahá in Green Acre

'Abdu'l-Bahá in Bennett house

into His presence; the poignant sight when He stooped low to the grave of His beloved disciple, Thornton Chase, in Inglewood Cemetery, and kissed his tombstone, an example which all those present hastened to follow; the distinguished gathering of Christians, Jews and Muslims, men and women and representative of both the East and the West, assembled to hear His discourse on world unity in the mosque at Woking—such scenes as these, even in the cold record of the printed page, must still have much of their original impressiveness and power.

'Abdu'l-Bahá with children

'Abdu'l-Bahá with friends, U.S.A.

‘Abdu’l-Bahá in Green Acre

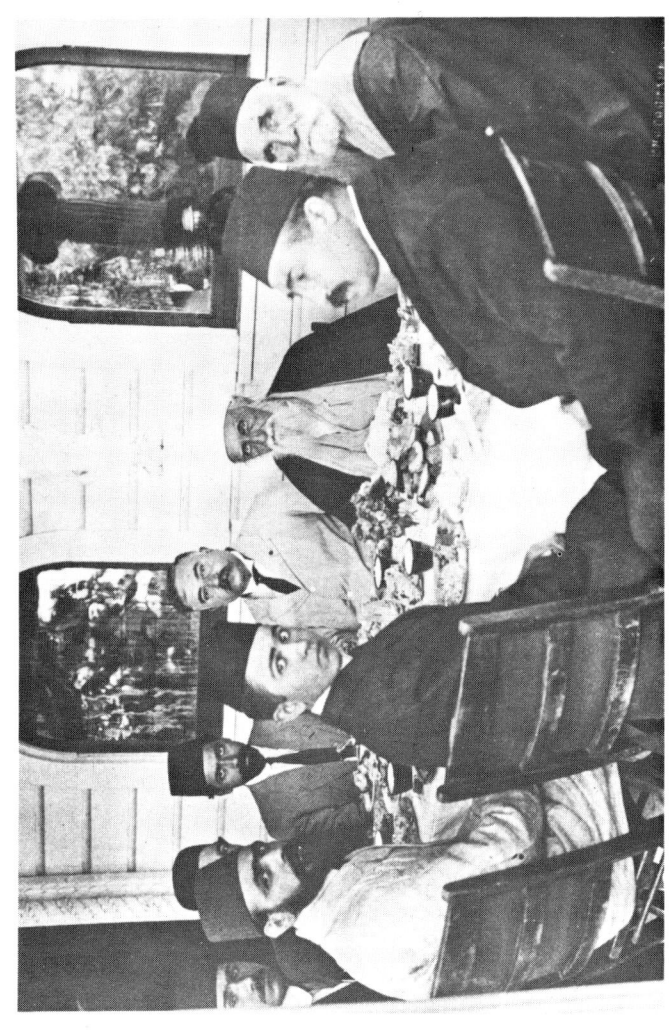

At barbeque in honour of 'Abdu'l-Bahá with Persian Consul-General Topakyan

WHO knows what thoughts flooded the heart of 'Abdu'l-Bahá as He found Himself the central figure of such memorable scenes as these? Who knows what thoughts were uppermost in His mind as He sat at breakfast beside the Lord Mayor of London, or was received with extraordinary deference by the Khedive himself in his palace, or as He listened to the cries of "Alláh-u-Abhá" and to the hymns of thanksgiving and praise that would herald His approach to the numerous and brilliant assemblages of His enthusiastic followers and friends organized in so many cities of the American continent? Who knows what memories stirred within Him as He stood before the thundering waters of Niagara, breathing the free air of a far distant land, or gazed, in the course of a brief and much-needed rest, upon the green woods and countryside in Glenwood Springs, or moved with a retinue of Oriental believers along the paths of the Trocadero gardens in Paris, or walked alone in the evening beside the majestic Hudson on Riverside Drive in New York, or as He paced the terrace of the Hotel du Parc at Thonon-les-Bains, overlooking the Lake of Geneva, or as He watched from Serpentine Bridge in London the pearly chain of Lights beneath the trees stretching as

'Abdu'l-Bahá seated in the garden of the home of Mrs McNutt

'Abdu'l-Bahá with Dr. and Mrs. Ali Kulí-Khán

'Abdu'l-Bahá with Rúhíyyih Jones and two daughters of M. Windust

far as the eye could see? Memories of the sorrows, the poverty, the overhanging doom of His earlier years; memories of His mother who sold her gold buttons to provide Him, His brother and His sister with sustenance, and who was forced, in her darkest hours, to place a handful of dry flour in the palm of His hand to appease His hunger; of His own childhood when pursued and derided by a mob of ruffians in the streets of Ṭihrán; of the damp and gloomy room, formerly a morgue, which He occupied in the barracks of 'Akká and of His imprisonment in the dungeon of that city—memories such as these must surely have thronged His mind. Thoughts, too, must have visited Him of the Báb's captivity in the mountain fastnesses of Ádhirbáyján, when at night time He was refused even a lamp, and of His cruel and tragic execution when hundreds of bullets riddled His youthful breast. Above all His thoughts must have centred on Bahá'u'lláh, Whom He loved so passionately and Whose trials He had witnessed and had shared from His boyhood. The vermin-infested Síyáh-Chál of Ṭihrán; the bastinado inflicted upon Him in Ámul; the humble fare which filled His Kashkúl while He lived for two years the life of a dervish in the mountains of Kurdistán; the days in Baghdád when He did not even possess a change of linen, and when His followers subsisted on a handful of dates; His confinement behind the prison-walls of 'Akká, when for nine years even the sight of verdure was denied Him; and the public humiliation to which He was subjected at government headquarters in that city—pictures from the tragic past such as these must have many a time overpowered Him with feelings of mingled gratitude and sorrow, as He witnessed the many marks of respect, of esteem, and honour now shown Him and the Faith which He represented. "*O Bahá'u'lláh! What hast Thou done?*" He, as reported by the chronicler of His travels, was heard to exclaim one evening as He was being swiftly driven to fulfil His third engagement of the day in Washington, "*O Bahá'u'lláh! May my life be sacrificed for Thee! O Bahá'u'lláh! May my soul be offered up for Thy sake! How full were Thy days with trials and tribulations! How severe the ordeals Thou didst endure! How solid the foundation Thou hast finally laid, and how glorious the banner Thou didst hoist!*" "One day, as He was strolling," that same chronicler has testified, "He called to remembrance the days of the Blessed Beauty, referring with sadness to His sojourn in Suláymáníyyih, to His loneliness and to the wrongs inflicted upon Him. Though He had often recounted that episode, that day He was so overcome with emotion that He sobbed aloud in His grief . . . All His attendants wept with Him, and were plunged into sorrow as they heard the tale of the woeful trials endured by the Ancient Beauty, and witnessed the tenderness of heart manifested by His Son."

A most significant scene in a century-old drama had been enacted. A glorious chapter in the history of the first Bahá'í century had been written. Seeds of undreamt-of potentialities had,

'Abdu'l-Bahá in Lincoln Park, Chicago

'Abdu'l-Bahá with Rúhíyyih Jones

'Abdu'l-Bahá walking on Riverside Drive, New York City

'Abdu'l-Bahá with an American family

with the hand of the Centre of the Covenant Himself, been sown in some of the fertile fields of the Western world. Never in the entire range of religious history had any Figure of comparable stature arisen to perform a labour of such magnitude and imperishable worth. Forces were unleashed through those fateful journeys which even now . . . we are unable to measure or comprehend. Already a Queen, inspired by the powerful arguments adduced by 'Abdu'l-Bahá in the course of His addresses in support of the Divinity of Muḥammad, has proclaimed her faith, and borne public testimony to the Divine origin of the Prophet of Islám. Already a President of the United States, imbibing some of the principles so clearly enunciated by Him in His discourses, has incorporated them in a Peace Programme which stands out as the boldest and noblest proposal yet made for the well-being and security of mankind. And already, alas! a world which proved deaf to His warnings and refused to heed His summons has plunged itself into two global wars of unprecedented severity, the repercussions of which none as yet can even dimly visualize.

Glimpses of His Talks and Writings

A meeting such as this seems like a beautiful cluster of precious jewels—pearls, rubies, diamonds, sapphires. It is a source of joy and delight. Whatever is conducive to the unity of the world of mankind is most acceptable and praiseworthy; whatever is the cause of discord and disunion is saddening and deplorable. Consider the significance of unity and harmony.

This evening I will speak to you upon the subject of existence and non-existence, life and death. Existence is the expression and outcome of composition and combination. Non-existence is the expression and outcome of division and disintegration. If we study the forms of existence in the material universe, we find that all created things are the result of composition. Material elements have grouped together in infinite variety and endless forms. Each organism is a compound; each object is an expression of elemental affinity. We find the complex human organism simply an aggregation of cellular structure; the tree is a composite of plant cells; the animal a combination and grouping of cellular atoms or units, and so on. Existence or the expression of being is therefore composition, and non-existence is decomposition, division, disintegration. When elements have been brought

'Abdu'l-Bahá with Rúhíyyih Jones and Joseph Ioas

'Abdu'l-Bahá leading Rúhíyyih Jones to the light

'Abdu'l-Bahá at banquet at Great Northern Hotel, New York City, 23 November 1912

'Abdu'l-Bahá in Mr. Milburn's church, Chicago, 1912

together in a certain plan of combination the result is the human organism; when these elements separate and disperse, the outcome is death and non-existence. Life is therefore the product of composition, and death signifies decomposition.

Likewise in the world of minds and souls, fellowship, which is an expression of composition, is conductive to life; whereas discord, which is an expression of decomposition, is the equivalent of death. Without cohesion among the individual elements which compose the body-politic, disintegration and decay must inevitably follow and life be extinguished. Ferocious animals have no fellowship. The vultures and tigers are solitary whereas domestic animals live together in complete harmony. The sheep, black and white, associate without discord. Birds of various species and colours wing their flight and feed together without trace of enmity or disagreement. Therefore in the world of humanity it is wise and seemly that all the individual members should manifest unity and affinity. In the clustered jewels of the races, may the coloured people be as sapphires and rubies, and the whites as diamonds and pearls. The composite beauty of humanity will be witnessed in their unity and blending. How glorious the spectacle of real unity among mankind! How conducive to peace, confidence and happiness if races and nations were united in fellowship and accord! The prophets of God were sent into the world upon this mission of unity and agreement; that these long-separated sheep might flock together. When the sheep separate they are exposed to danger, but in a flock and under protection of the shepherd they are safe from the attack of all ferocious enemies.

When the racial elements of the American nation unite in actual fellowship and accord, the lights of the oneness of humanity will shine, the day of eternal glory and bliss will dawn, the spirit of God encompass and the divine favours descend. Under the leadership and training of God the real shepherd, all will be protected and preserved. He will lead them in green pastures of happiness and sustenance and they will attain to the real goal of existence. This is the blessing and benefit of unity; this is the outcome of love. This is the sign of the "Most Great Peace"; this is the star of the oneness of the human world. Consider how blessed this condition will be. I pray for you and ask the confirmation and assistance of God in your behalf.

(*Talk given by 'Abdu'l-Bahá, 24 April 1912, Washington, D.C.*)

TONIGHT I am very happy for I have come here to meet my friends. I consider you my relatives, my companions; and I am your comrade.

You must be thankful to God that you are poor, for His Holiness Jesus Christ has said "Blessed are the poor"; He never said blessed are the rich. He said too that the Kingdom is for the poor and that it is easier for a camel to enter a needle's eye than for a rich man to enter God's Kingdom. Therefore you must be thankful to God that although in this world you are indigent, yet the treasures of God are within your reach; and although in the material realms you are poor, yet in the Kingdom of God you are precious. His Holiness Jesus Himself was poor. He did not belong to the rich. He passed His time in the desert travelling among the poor, and lived upon the herbs of the field. He had no place to lay His head; no home. He was exposed in the open to heat, cold and frost; to inclement weather of all kinds, yet He chose this rather than riches. If riches were considered a glory the prophet Moses would have chosen them; Jesus would have been a rich man. When Jesus Christ appeared it was the poor who first accepted Him, not the rich. Therefore you are the disciples of Jesus Christ; you are His comrades for He outwardly was poor not rich. Even this earth's happiness does not depend upon wealth. You will find many of the wealthy exposed to dangers and troubled by difficulties, and in their last moments upon the bed of death there remains the regret that they must be separated from that to which their hearts are so attached. They come into this world naked and they must go from it naked. All they possess they must leave behind and pass away solitary, alone. Often at the time of death their souls are filled with remorse, and worst of all, their hope in the mercy of God is less than ours. Praise be to God! Our hope is in the mercy of God and there is no doubt that the divine compassion is bestowed upon the poor. His Holiness Jesus Christ said so; His holiness Bahá'u'lláh said so. While Bahá'u'lláh was in Baghdád, still in possession of great wealth, He left all He had and went alone from the city, living two years among the poor. They were His comrades. He ate with them, slept with them and gloried in being one of them. He chose for one of His names the title of "The Poor One", and often in His writings refers to Himself as "Dervish", which in Persian means "poor"; and of this title He was very proud. He admonished all that we must be the servants of the poor, helpers of the poor, remember the sorrows of the poor, associate with them for thereby we may inherit the Kingdom of Heaven. God has not said that there are mansions prepared for us if we pass our time associating with the rich but He has said there are many mansions prepared

'Abdu'l-Bahá in America

'Abdu'l-Bahá with group in West Englewood, New Jersey, America, 1912

'Abdu'l-Bahá with Eastern friends at the Shrine of the Báb

for the servants of the poor, for the poor are very dear to God. The mercies and bounties of God are with them. The rich are mostly negligent, inattentive, steeped in worldliness, depending upon their means, whereas the poor are dependent upon God and their reliance is upon him, not upon themselves. Therefore the poor are nearer the threshold of God and His throne.

Jesus was a poor man. One night when He was out in the fields the rain began to fall. He had no place to go for shelter so He lifted His eyes toward Heaven saying "O Father! for the birds of the air Thou hast created nests, for the sheep a fold, for the animals dens, for the fishes places of refuge, but for me Thou hast provided no shelter; there is no place where I may lay my head; my bed consists of the cold ground, my lamps at night are the stars and my food is the grass of the field, yet who upon earth is richer than I? For the greatest blessing Thou hast not given to the rich and mighty but unto me for Thou hast given me the poor. To me Thou hast granted this blessing. They are mine. Therefore am I the richest man on earth."

So my comrades you are following in the footsteps of Jesus Christ. Your lives are similar to His life, your attitude is like unto Him, you resemble Him more than the rich. Therefore we will thank God that we have been so blest with real riches. And in conclusion I ask you to accept 'Abdu'l-Bahá as your servant.

(*Talk given by 'Abdu'l-Bahá, 19 April 1912, New York*)

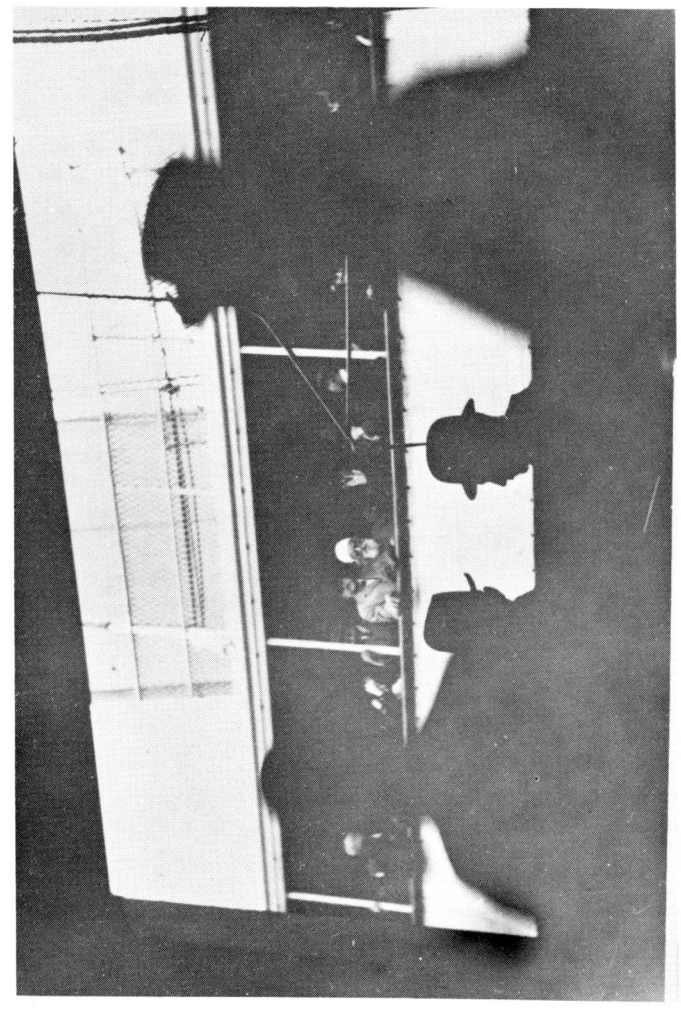

'Abdu'l-Bahá leaving New York City on the "Celtic", December 1912

'Abdu'l-Bahá kissing Sarah Farmer

'Abdu'l-Bahá in West Englewood, New Jersey, 1912

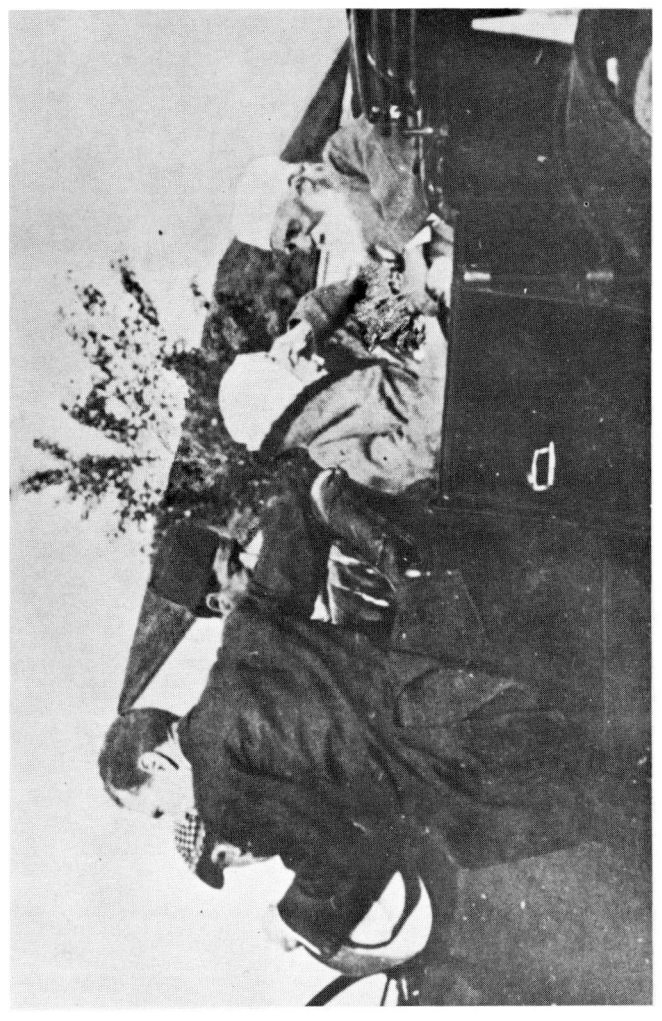

'Abdu'l-Bahá and Sarah Farmer, Green Acre, 1912

NOBLE friends, seekers after God! Praise be to God! Today the light of Truth is shining upon the world in its abundance; the breezes of the heavenly garden are blowing throughout all regions; the call of the Kingdom is heard in all lands, and the breath of the Holy Spirit is felt in all hearts that are faithful. The Spirit of God is giving eternal life. In this wonderful age the East is enlightened, the West is fragrant, and everywhere the soul inhales the holy perfume. The sea of the unity of mankind is lifting up its waves with joy, for there is real communication between the hearts and minds of men. The banner of the Holy Spirit is uplifted, and men see it, and are assured with the knowledge that this is a new day.

This is a new cycle of human power. All the horizons of the world are luminous, and the world will become indeed as a garden and a paradise. It is the hour of unity of the sons of men and of the drawing together of all races and all classes. You are loosed from ancient superstitions which have kept men ignorant, destroying the foundations of true humanity.

The gift of God to this enlightened age is the knowledge of the oneness of mankind and of the fundamental oneness of religion. War shall cease between nations, and by the Will of God the

'Abdu'l-Bahá at boys' camp

*Taken at Dr. Henderson's camp for boys, near Dublin, New Hampshire,
1 August 1912*

Taken at the Wilhelm home, West England, New Jersey, about June 1912

'Abdu'l-Bahá at dedication of Temple site in Wilmette, Illinois, 1912

Most Great Peace shall come; the world will be seen as a new world, and all men will live as brothers.

In the days of old an instinct for warfare was developed in the struggle with wild animals; this is no longer necessary; nay, rather, co-operation and mutual understanding are seen to produce the greatest welfare of mankind. Enmity is now the result of prejudice only.

In the "Hidden Words" Bahá'u'lláh says, "Justice is to be loved above all." Praise be to God, in this country the standard of justice has been raised; a great effort is being made to give all souls an equal and true place. This is the desire of all noble natures; this is today the teaching for the East and for the West; therefore the East and the West will understand each other and reverence each other, and embrace like long-parted lovers who have found each other.

There is one God; mankind is one; the foundations of religion are one. Let us worship Him, and give praise for all His great Prophets and Messengers who have manifested His brightness and glory.

The blessing of the Eternal One be with you in all its richness, that each soul according to his measure may take freely of him. Amen.

(*Talk given by 'Abdu'l-Bahá, 1911, London*)

'*Abdu'l-Bahá with young man breaking ground at Temple land, Chicago, 1912*

DO you know in what Day you are living? Do you realize in what Dispensation you are alive? Have you not heard in the Holy Scriptures that at the consummation of the ages there shall appear a Day which is the Sun of all the past days? This is the Day in which the Lord of Hosts has come down from Heaven on the clouds of glory! This is the Day in which the inhabitants of all the world shall enter under the shelter of the Word of God.

This is the Day whose real sovereign is His Highness the Almighty. This is the Day when the East and the West shall embrace each other like unto two lovers. This is the Day in which war and contention shall be forgotten. This is the Day in which nations and governments will enter into an eternal bond of amity and conciliation. This Century is the fulfilment of the Promised Century.

This Day is the dawn of the appearances of the traces of the glorious visions of the past prophets and sages.

Now is the dawn; ere long the effulgent Sun shall rise and station itself in the meridian of

'Abdu'l-Bahá laying cornerstone of House of Worship, Wilmette, 1912

its majesty. Then you shall observe the effects of the Sun. Then you shall behold what heavenly illumination has become manifest. Then you shall comprehend that these are the infinite bestowals of God! Then you shall see that this world has become another world. Then you shall perceive that the Teachings of God have universally spread.

Rest ye assured that this darkness shall be dispelled and these impenetrable clouds which have darkened the horizon shall be scattered, and the Sun of Reality shall appear in its full splendour. Its rays shall melt the icebergs of hatred and differences which have transformed the moving sea of humanity into hard-frozen immensity. The vices of the world of nature shall be changed into praiseworthy attributes, and the lights of the excellences of the Divine realm shall appear.

The principles of Bahá'u'lláh, like unto the spirit, shall penetrate the dead body of the world, and the Love of God, like unto an artery, shall beat through the heart of the five continents.

The East shall become illumined, the West perfumed, and the children of men enter beneath the all-embracing canopy of the oneness of the world of humanity.

In this Day the rest of the people are asleep. Praise be to God that you are awakened! They

'Abdu'l-Bahá on way to Knighthood ceremony, 1920

are all uninformed, but praise be to God you are informed of the mysteries of God! Thank ye God that in this arena you have preceded others. I hope that each one of you may become a pillar of the palace of the oneness of the world of humanity. May each one of you become a luminous star of this heaven, thus lighting the path of those who are seeking the goal of human perfection.

(*Talk given by* '*Abdu'l-Bahá, 1913, Paris, France*)

'Abdu'l-Bahá, Knighthood ceremony, 1920

OH, how I long that it could be made possible for me to travel through these parts, even if necessary on foot and with the utmost poverty, and while passing through the cities, villages, mountains, deserts and oceans, cry at the top of my voice "Ya-Bahá'u'l-Abhá!" and promote the divine teachings. But now this is not feasible for me; therefore I live in great regret; perchance, God willing, ye may become assisted therein.

* * *

You have observed that while 'Abdu'l-Bahá was in the utmost bodily weakness and feebleness, while He was indisposed, and had not the power to move—notwithstanding this physical state He travelled through many countries, in Europe and America, and in churches, meetings and conventions, was occupied with the promotion of the divine principles and summoned the people to the manifestation of the Kingdom of Abhá. You have also observed how the confirmations of the Blessed Perfection encompassed all. What result is forthcoming from material rest, tranquillity, luxury and attachment to this corporeal world! It is evident that the man who pursues these things will in the end become afflicted with regret and loss.

Taken in Haifa, February 1919

Consequently, one must close his eyes wholly to these thoughts, long for eternal life, the sublimity of the world of humanity, the celestial developments, the Holy Spirit, the promotion of the Word of God, the guidance of the inhabitants of the globe, the promulgation of Universal Peace and the proclamation of the oneness of the world of humanity! *This is the work!* Otherwise like unto other animals and birds one must occupy himself with the requirements of this physical life, the satisfaction of which is the highest aspiration of the animal kingdom, and one must stalk across the earth like unto the quadrupeds.

Consider ye! No matter how much man gains wealth, riches and opulence in this world, he will not become as independent as a cow. For these fattened cows roam freely over the vast tableland. All the prairies and meadows are theirs for grazing, and all the springs and rivers are theirs for drinking! No matter how much they graze, the fields will not be exhausted! It is evident that they have earned these material bounties with the utmost facility.

Still more ideal than this life is the life of the bird. A bird, on the summit of a mountain, on the high, waving branches, has built for itself a nest more beautiful than the palaces of the kings! The air is in the utmost purity, the water cool and clear as crystal, the panorama charming and enchanting. In such glorious surroundings, he expends his numbered days. All the harvests of the plain are his possessions, having earned all

'Abdu'l-Bahá with pilgrims at No. 7 Haparsim Street

this wealth without the least labour. Hence, no matter how much man may advance in this world, he shall not attain to the station of this bird! Thus it becomes evident that in the matters of this world, however much man may strive and work to the point of death, he will be unable to earn the abundance, the freedom and the independent life of a small bird. This proves and establishes the fact that man is not created for the life of this ephemeral world: nay, rather, is he created for the acquirement of infinite perfections, for the attainment to the sublimity of the world of humanity, to be drawn nigh unto the divine threshold, and to sit on the throne of everlasting sovereignty!

Upon you be Bahá El-Abhá!

Any soul starting on a trip of teaching to various parts, and while sojourning in strange countries, may peruse the following supplication—day and night.

O God! O God! Thou seest me enamoured and attracted toward Thy Kingdom, the El-Abhá, enkindled with the fire of Thy love amongst mankind, a herald of Thy Kingdom in these vast and spacious countries, severed from aught else save Thee, relying on Thee, abandoning rest and comfort, remote from my native home, a wanderer in these regions, a stranger fallen on the ground, humble before Thy exalted threshold, submissive toward Thy most high realm, supplicating Thee

'Abdu'l-Bahá riding on donkey accompanied by two friends

in the middle of nights and in the heart of evenings, entreating and invoking Thee in the morn and eve,—so that Thou mayest assist me in the service of Thy Cause, the promotion of Thy Teachings and the exaltation of Thy Word in the Easts of the earth and the Wests thereof.

O Lord! Strengthen my back and confirm me in Thy servitude with all my powers, and do not leave me alone and by myself in these countries.

O Lord! Associate with me in my loneliness and accompany me in my journeys through these foreign lands.

Verily, Thou art the confirmer of whomsoever Thou Willest in that which Thou desirest, and verily Thou art the Powerful, the Omnipotent.

ye kind friends! Uplift your magnanimity and soar high toward the apex of heaven so that your blessed hearts may become illumined more and more, day by day, through the Rays of the Sun of Reality, that is, His Holiness Bahá'u'lláh; at every moment the spirits may obtain a new life, and the darkness of the world of nature may be entirely dispelled; thus you may become incarnate light and personified spirit, become entirely unaware of the sordid matters of this world and in touch with the affairs of the divine world.

Behold the portals which Bahá'u'lláh hath opened before you! Consider how exalted and lofty is the station you are destined to attain; how unique the favours with which you have been endowed. Should we become intoxicated with this cup, the sovereignty of this globe of earth will become lower in our estimation than the children's plays. Should they place in the arena the crown of the government of the whole world, and invited each one of us to accept it, undoubtedly we shall not condescend, and shall refuse to accept it.

To attain to this supreme station is, however, dependent on the realization of certain conditions:

The first condition is firmness in the Covenant

'Abdu'l-Bahá in Germany

of God. For the power of the Covenant will protect the Cause of Bahá'u'lláh from the doubts of the people of error. It is the fortified fortress of the Cause of God and the firm pillar of the religion of God. Today no power can conserve the oneness of the Bahá'í world save the Covenant of God; otherwise differences like unto a most great tempest will encompass the Bahá'í world. It is undubitably clear that the pivot of the oneness of mankind is nothing else but the power of the Covenant. Had the Covenant not come to pass, had it not been revealed from the Supreme Pen and had not the Book of the Covenant, like unto the ray of the Sun of Reality, illuminated the world, the forces of the Cause of God would have been utterly scattered and certain souls who were the prisoners of their own passions and lusts would have taken into their hands an axe, cutting the root of this Blessed Tree. Every person would have pushed forward his own desire and every individual aired his own opinion! Notwithstanding this great Covenant, a few negligent souls galloped with their chargers into the battlefield, thinking perchance they might be able to weaken the foundation of the Cause of God: but praise be to God all of them were afflicted with regret and loss, and ere long they shall see themselves in poignant despair. Therefore, in the beginning one must make his steps firm in the Covenant so that the confirmations of Bahá'u'lláh may encircle from all sides, the cohorts of the Supreme Concourse may become the supporters and the helpers, and the exhortations and advices of

'Abdu'l-Bahá, like unto the pictures engraved on stone, may remain permanent and ineffaceable in the tablets of the hearts.

The second condition: Fellowship and love amongst the believers. The divine friends must be attracted to and enamoured of each other and ever be ready and willing to sacrifice their own lives for each other. Should one soul from amongst the believers meet another, it must be as though a thirsty one with parched lips has reached to the fountain of the water of life, or a lover has met his true beloved. For one of the greatest divine wisdoms regarding the appearance of the Holy Manifestations is this: The souls may come to know each other and become intimate with each other; the power of the love of God may make all of them the waves of one sea, the flowers of one rose garden, and the stars of one heaven. This is the wisdom for the appearance of the Holy Manifestations! When the most great bestowal reveals itself in the hearts of the believers, the world of nature will be transformed, the darkness of the contingent being will vanish, and heavenly illumination will be obtained. Then the whole world will become the Paradise of Abhá, every one of the believers of God will become a blessed tree, producing wonderful fruits.

O ye friends! Fellowship, fellowship! Love, love! Unity, unity! So that the power of the Bahá'í Cause may appear and become manifest in the world of existence. My thoughts are turned towards you, and my heart leaps within me at

'Abdu'l-Bahá on Mount Carmel

your mention. Could ye know how my soul gloweth with your love, so great a happiness would flood your hearts as to cause you to become enamoured with each other.

The third condition: Teachers must continually travel to all parts of the continent, nay, rather to all parts of the world, but they must travel like 'Abdu'l-Bahá, who journeyed throughout the cities of America. He was sanctified and free from every attachment and in the utmost severance. Just as His Holiness Christ says, "Shake off the very dust from your feet."

You have observed that while in America many souls in the utmost of supplication and entreaty desired to offer some gifts, but this servant, in accord with the exhortations and behests of the Blessed Perfection, never accepted a thing, although on certain occasions we were in most straitened circumstances. But, on the other hand, if a soul for the sake of God, voluntarily and out of his pure desire, wishes to offer a contribution (toward the expenses of a teacher) in order to make the contributor happy, the teacher may accept a small sum, but must live with the utmost contentment.

The aim is this: The intention of the teacher must be pure, his heart independent, his spirit attracted, his thought at peace, his resolution firm, his magnanimity exalted and in the love of God a shining torch. Should he become as such, his sanctified breath will even affect the rock; otherwise there will be no result whatsoever. As long as a soul is not perfected, how can he efface

'Abdu'l-Bahá in garden at No. 7 Haparsim Street

the defects of others. Unless he is detached from aught else save God, how can he teach severance to others!

In short, O ye believers of God! Endeavour ye, so that you may take hold of every means in the promulgation of the religion of God and the diffusion of the fragrances of God.

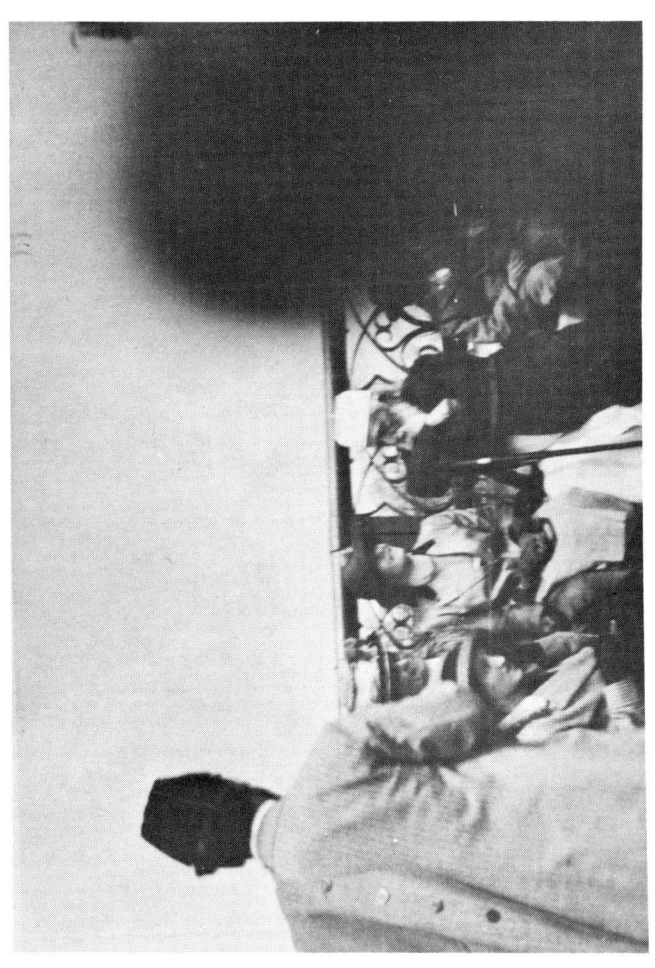

The War Years

THE war of 1914–18, repeatedly foreshadowed by 'Abdu'l-Bahá in the dark warnings He uttered in the course of His western travels, and which broke out eight months after His return to the Holy Land, once more cast a shadow of danger over His life, the last that was to darken the years of His agitated yet glorious ministry.

The late entry of the United States of America in that world-convulsing conflict, the neutrality of Persia, the remoteness of India and of the Far East from the theatre of operations, insured the protection of the overwhelming majority of His followers, who, though for the most part entirely cut off for a number of years from the spiritual centre of their Faith, were still able to conduct their affairs and safeguard the fruits of their recent achievements in comparative safety and freedom.

In the Holy Land, however, though the outcome of that tremendous struggle was to liberate once and for all the Heart and Centre of the Faith from the Turkish yoke, a yoke which had imposed for so long upon its Founder and His Successor such oppressive and humiliating restrictions, yet severe privations and grave dangers continued to surround its inhabitants during the major part of that conflict, and renewed, for a time, the perils

'Abdu'l-Bahá in England

which had confronted 'Abdu'l-Bahá during the years of His incarceration in 'Akká. The privations inflicted on the inhabitants by the gross incompetence, the shameful neglect, the cruelty and callous indifference of both the civil and military authorities, though greatly alleviated through the bountiful generosity, the foresight and the tender care of 'Abdu'l-Bahá, were aggravated by the rigours of a strict blockade. A bombardment of Haifa by the Allies was a constant threat, at one time so real that it necessitated the temporary removal of 'Abdu'l-Bahá, His family and members of the local community to the village of Abú-Sinán at the foot of the hills east of 'Akká. The Turkish Commander-in-Chief, the brutal, the all-powerful and unscrupulous Jamál Pá<u>sh</u>á, an inveterate enemy of the Faith, through his own ill-founded suspicions and the instigation of its enemies, had already grievously afflicted 'Abdu'l-Bahá, and even expressed his intention of crucifying Him and of razing to the ground the Tomb of Bahá'u'lláh. 'Abdu'l-Bahá Himself still suffered from the ill-health and exhaustion brought on by the fatigues of His three-year journeys. He felt acutely the virtual stoppage of all communication with most of the Bahá'í centres throughout the world. Agony filled His soul at the spectacle of human slaughter precipitated through humanity's failure to respond to the summons He had issued, or to heed the warnings He had given. Surely sorrow upon sorrow was added to the burden of trials and vicissitudes which He, since His boyhood, had borne so

'Abdu'l-Bahá on way to knighthood ceremony, 1920

heroically for the sake, and in the service, of His Father's Cause.

And yet during these sombre days, the darkness of which was reminiscent of the tribulations endured during the most dangerous period of His incarceration in the prison-fortress of 'Akká, 'Abdu'l-Bahá, whilst in the precincts of His Father's Shrine, or when dwelling in the House He occupied in 'Akká, or under the shadow of the Báb's sepulchre on Mt. Carmel, was moved to confer once again, and for the last time in His life, on the community of His American followers a signal mark of His special favour by investing them, on the eve of the termination of His earthly ministry, through the revelation of the Tablets of the Divine Plan, with a world mission, whose full implications even now . . . still remain undisclosed, and whose unfoldment thus far, though as yet in its initial stages, has so greatly enriched the spiritual as well as the administrative annals of the first Bahá'í century.

The conclusion of this terrible conflict, the first stage in a titanic convulsion long predicted by Bahá'u'lláh, not only marked the extinction of Turkish rule in the Holy Land and sealed the doom of that military despot who had vowed to destroy 'Abdu'l-Bahá, but also shattered once and for all the last hopes still entertained by the remnant of Covenant-breakers who, untaught by the severe retribution that had already overtaken them, still aspired to witness the extinction of the light of Bahá'u'lláh's Covenant. Furthermore, it produced those revolutionary changes which, on

'Abdu'l-Bahá on terrace in front of the Shrine of the Báb

the one hand, fulfilled the ominous predictions made by Bahá'u'lláh in the Kitáb-i-Aqdas, and enabled, according to Scriptural prophecy, so large an element of the *"outcasts of Israel,"* the *"remnant"* of the *"flock,"* to *"assemble"* in the Holy Land, and to be brought back to *"their folds"* and *"their own border,"* beneath the shadow of the *"Incomparable Branch,"* referred to by 'Abdu'l-Bahá in His "Some Answered Questions," and which, on the other hand, gave birth to the institution of the League of Nations, the precursor of that World Tribunal which, as prophesied by that same "Incomparable Branch," the peoples and nations of the earth must needs unitedly establish.

No need to dwell on the energetic steps which the English believers as soon as they had been apprized of the dire peril threatening the life of 'Abdu'l-Bahá undertook to insure His security; on the measures independently taken whereby Lord Curzon and others in the British Cabinet were advised as to the critical situation at Haifa; on the prompt intervention of Lord Lamington, who immediately wrote to the Foreign Office to "explain the importance of 'Abdu'l-Bahá's position;" on the despatch which the Foreign Secretary, Lord Balfour, on the day of the receipt of this letter, sent to General Allenby, instructing him to "extend every protection and consideration to 'Abdu'l-Bahá, His family and His friends;" on the cablegram subsequently sent by the General, after the capture of Haifa, to

'Abdu'l-Bahá, Knighthood ceremony, 1920

London, requesting the authorities to "notify the world that 'Abdu'l-Bahá is safe;" on the orders which that same General issued to the General Commanding Officer in command of the Haifa operations to insure 'Abdu'l-Bahá's safety, thus frustrating the express intention of the Turkish Commander-in-Chief (according to information which had reached the British Intelligence Service) to "crucify 'Abdu'l-Bahá and His family on Mt. Carmel" in the event of the Turkish army being compelled to evacuate Haifa and retreat northwards.

The three years which elapsed between the liberation of Palestine by the British forces and the passing of 'Abdu'l-Bahá were marked by a further enhancement of the prestige which the Faith, despite the persecutions to which it had been subjected, had acquired at its world centre, and by a still greater extension in the range of its teaching activities in various parts of the world. The danger which, for no less than three score years and five, had threatened the lives of the Founders of the Faith and of the Centre of His Covenant, was now at long last through the instrumentality of that war completely and definitely lifted. The Head of the Faith, and its twin holy Shrines, in the plain of 'Akká and on the slopes of Mt. Carmel, were henceforth to enjoy for the first time, through the substitution of a new and liberal régime for the corrupt administration of the past, a freedom from restrictions which was later expanded into a

'Abdu'l-Bahá being knighted

clearer recognition of the institutions of the Cause. Nor were the British authorities slow to express their appreciation of the rôle which 'Abdu'l-Bahá had played in allaying the burden of suffering that had oppressed the inhabitants of the Holy Land during the dark days of that distressing conflict. The conferment of a knighthood upon Him at a ceremony specially held for His sake in Haifa, at the residence of the British Governor, at which notables of various communities had assembled; the visit paid Him by General and Lady Allenby, who were His guests at luncheon in Bahjí, and whom He conducted to the Tomb of Bahá'u'lláh; the interview at His Haifa residence between Him and King Feisal who shortly after became the ruler of 'Iráq; the several calls paid Him by Sir Herbert Samuel (later Viscount Samuel of Carmel) both before and after his appointment as High Commissioner for Palestine; His meeting with Lord Lamington who, likewise, called upon Him in Haifa, as well as with the then Governor of Jerusalem, Sir Ronald Storrs; the multiplying evidences of the recognition of His high and unique position by all religious communities, whether Muslim, Christian or Jewish; the influx of pilgrims who, from East and West, flocked to the Holy Land in comparative ease and safety to visit the Holy Tombs in 'Akká and Haifa, to pay their share of homage to Him, to celebrate the signal protection vouchsafed by Providence to the Faith and its followers, and to give thanks for the final emancipation of its Head and world Centre from Turkish yoke—these

contributed, each in its own way, to heighten the prestige which the Faith of Bahá'u'lláh had been steadily and gradually acquiring through the inspired leadership of 'Abdu'l-Bahá.

REGARD not the person of 'Abdu'l-Bahá, for He will eventually take His leave of you all; nay, fix your gaze upon the Word of God . . . The loved ones of God must arise with such steadfastness that should, in one moment, hundreds of souls even as 'Abdu'l-Bahá Himself be made a target for the darts of woe, nothing whatsoever shall affect or lessen their . . . service to the Cause of God.

The Passing of 'Abdu'l-Bahá

'ABDU'L-BAHÁ's great work was now ended. The historic Mission with which His Father had, twenty-nine years previously, invested Him had been gloriously consummated. A memorable chapter in the history of the first Bahá'í century had been written. The Heroic Age of the Bahá'í Dispensation, in which He had participated since its inception, and played so unique a rôle, had drawn to a close. He had suffered as no disciple of the Faith, who had drained the cup of martyrdom, had suffered, He had laboured as none of its greatest heroes had laboured. He had witnessed triumphs such as neither the Herald of the Faith nor its Author had ever witnessed.

At the close of His strenuous Western tours, which had called forth the last ounce of His ebbing strength, He had written: *"Friends, the time is coming when I shall be no longer with you. I have done all that could be done. I have served the Cause of Bahá'u'lláh to the utmost of My ability. I have laboured night and day all the years of My life. O how I long to see the believers shouldering the responsibilities of the Cause! . . . My days are numbered, and save this there remains none other joy for me."* Several years before He had thus alluded to His passing: *"O ye My faithful loved ones! Should at any time afflicting events come to pass in the Holy Land, never feel*

At No. 7 Haparsim Street

disturbed or agitated. Fear not, neither grieve. For whatsoever thing happeneth will cause the Word of God to be exalted, and His Divine fragrances to be diffused." And again: "*Remember, whether or not I be on earth, My presence will be with you always.*"

In a Tablet addressed to the American believers, a few days before He passed away, He thus vented His pent-up longing to depart from this world: "*I have renounced the world and the people thereof . . . In the cage of this world I flutter even as a frightened bird, and yearn every day to take My flight unto Thy Kingdom. Yá Bahá'u'l-Abhá! Make Me drink of the cup of sacrifice, and set Me free.*" He revealed a prayer less than six months before His ascension in honour of a kinsman of the Báb, and in it wrote: "'*O Lord! My bones are weakened, and the hoar hairs glisten on my head . . . and I have now reached old age, failing in my powers.' . . . No strength is there left in Me wherewith to arise and serve Thy loved ones . . . O Lord, My Lord! Hasten My ascension unto Thy sublime Threshold . . . and My arrival at the Door of Thy grace beneath the shadow of Thy most great mercy . . .*"

Through the dreams He dreamed, through the conversations He held, through the Tablets He revealed, it became increasingly evident that His end was fast approaching. Two months before His passing He told His family of a dream he had had. "*I seemed,*" He said, "*to be standing within a great mosque, in the inmost shrine, facing the Qiblih, in the place of the Imám himself. I became aware that a large number of people were flocking into the mosque. More and yet more crowded in,*

taking their places in rows behind Me, until there was a vast multitude. As I stood I raised loudly the call to prayer. Suddenly the thought came to Me to go forth from the mosque. When I found Myself outside I said within Myself: 'For what reason came I forth, not having led the prayer? But it matters not; now that I have uttered the Call to prayer, the vast multitude will of themselves chant the prayer'." A few weeks later, whilst occupying a solitary room in the garden of His house, He recounted another dream to those around Him. "*I dreamed a dream,*" He said, "*and behold, the Blessed Beauty (Bahá'u'lláh) came and said to Me: 'Destroy this room'.*" None of those present comprehended the significance of this dream until He Himself had soon after passed away, when it became clear to them all that by the "room" was meant the temple of His body.

'Abdu'l-Bahá coming to Pilgrim House, 19 November 1921

'Abdu'l-Bahá in garden at No. 7 Haparsim Street

'Abdu'l-Bahá and friends in horse-drawn carriage

ON the last Friday morning of His stay on earth (25 November) He said to His daughters: "The wedding of <u>Kh</u>usraw must take place today. If you are too much occupied, I myself will make the necessary preparations, for it must take place this day." (<u>Kh</u>usraw was one of the favoured and trusted servants of the Master's Household.)

'Abdu'l-Bahá attended the noonday prayer at the Mosque. When He came out He found the poor waiting for the alms, which it was His custom to give every Friday. This day, as usual, He stood, in spite of very great fatigue, whilst He gave a coin to every one with His own hands.

After lunch He dictated some Tablets. His last ones. . . . When He had rested He walked in the garden. He seemed to be in a deep reverie.

His good and faithful servant, Ismá'íl Áqá, relates the following:

Some time about twenty days before my Master passed away I was near the garden when I heard Him summon an old believer saying:

"Come with me that we may admire together the beauty of the garden. Behold, what the spirit of devotion is able to achieve! This

flourishing place was, a few years ago, but a heap of stones, and now it is verdant with foliage and flowers. My desire is that after I am gone the loved ones may all arise to serve the Divine Cause and, please God, so shall be. Ere long men will arise who shall bring life to the world."

A few days after this He said: "I am so fatigued! The hour is come when I must leave everything and take my flight. I am too weary to walk." Then He said: "It was during the closing days of the Blessed Beauty, when I was engaged in gathering together His papers, which were strewn over the sofa in His writing chamber in Bahjí that He turned to me and said: 'It is of no use to gather them, I must leave them and flee away.'

"I also have finished my work, I can do nothing more. Therefore must I leave it, and take my departure."

Three days before His ascension, whilst seated in the garden, He called me and said, "I am sick with fatigue. Bring two of your oranges for me that I may eat them for your sake." This I did, and He having eaten them turned to me, saying, "Have you any of your sweet lemons?" He bade me fetch a few . . . Whilst I was plucking them, He came over to the tree saying, "Nay, but I must gather them with my own hands." Having eaten of the fruit He turned to me and asked, "Do you desire anything more?" Then with a pathetic gesture of His hands,

He touchingly, emphatically and deliberately said:

"Now it is finished, it is finished!"

These significant words penetrated my very soul. I felt each time He uttered them as if a knife were struck into my heart. I understood His meaning but never dreamed His end was so nigh.

Later in the evening of Friday He blessed the bride and bridegroom who had just been married. He spoke impressively to them. "K͟husraw," He said, "you have spent your childhood and youth in the service of this house; it is my hope that you will grow old under the same roof, ever and always serving God."

During the evening He attended the usual meeting of the friends in His own audience chamber.

In the morning of Saturday He arose early, came to the tea-room and had some tea. He asked for the fur-lined coat which had belonged to Bahá'u'lláh. He often put on this coat when He was cold or did not feel well. He so loved it. He then withdrew to His room, lay down on His bed and said, "Cover me up. I am very cold. Last night I did not sleep well, I felt cold. This is serious, it is the beginning."

After more blankets had been put on, He asked for the fur coat He had taken off to be placed over Him. That day He was rather feverish. In the evening His temperature rose still higher, but during the night the fever left Him. After midnight He asked for some tea.

'Abdu'l-Bahá at Stanford University

On Sunday morning He said: "I am quite well and will get up as usual and have tea with you in the tea-room." After He had dressed He was persuaded to remain on the sofa in His room. In the afternoon He sent all the friends up to the tomb of the Báb, where, on the occasion of the anniversary of the declaration of the Covenant a feast was being held, offered by a Pársi pilgrim who had lately arrived from India. At four in the afternoon, being on the sofa in His room, He said: "Ask my sister and all the family to come and have tea with me." After tea the Muftí of Haifa and the head of the Municipality, with another visitor, were received by Him. They remained about an hour. He spoke to them about Bahá'u'lláh, related to them His second dream, showed them extraordinary kindness and even more than his usual courtesy. He then bade them farewell, walking with them to the outer door in spite of their pleading that He should remain resting on His sofa. He then received a visit from the head of the police, an Englishman, who, too, had his share of the Master's gracious kindness. To him He gave some silk hand-woven Persian handkerchiefs which he very greatly appreciated.

. . . The same evening He asked after the health of every member of the Household, of the pilgrims and of the friends in Haifa. "Very good, very good," He said when told that none were ill. This was His very last utterance concerning His friends.

At eight in the evening He retired to bed, after taking a little nourishment, saying:

"I am quite well." He told all the family to go to bed and rest. Two of His daughters however stayed with Him. That night the Master had gone to sleep very calmly, quite free from fever. He awoke about 1.15 a.m., got up, and walked across to a table where He drank some water. He took off an outer night garment, saying:

"I am too warm." He went back to bed and when His daughter Ruhá K͟hánum, later on approached, she found Him lying peacefully and, as He looked into her face, He asked her to lift up the net curtains, saying:

"I have difficulty in breathing, give me more air." Some rose-water was brought to Him, of which he drank, sitting up in bed to do so, without any help. He again lay down, and as some food was offered Him, He remarked in a clear and distinct voice:

"You wish me to take some food, and I am going?" He gave them a beautiful look. His face was so calm, His expression so serene, they thought Him asleep.

He had gone from the gaze of His loved ones!

The eyes that had always looked out with loving kindness upon humanity, whether friends or foes, were now closed. The hands that had ever been stretched forth to give alms to the poor and the needy, the halt and the maimed, the blind, the orphan and the widow, had now

Funeral of 'Abdu'l-Bahá, 1921

At funeral of 'Abdu'l-Bahá, 1921

Funeral of 'Abdu'l-Bahá

finished their labour. The feet that, with untiring zeal, had gone upon the ceaseless errands of the Lord of Compassion were now at rest. The lips that had so eloquently championed the cause of the suffering sons of men, were now hushed in silence. The heart that had so powerfully throbbed with wondrous love for the children of God was now stilled. His glorious spirit had passed from the life on earth, from the persecutions of the enemies of righteousness, from the storm and stress of well nigh eighty years of indefatigable toil for the good of others.

His long martyrdom was ended!

Whilst yet the gloom of their bereavement was hanging darkly over disconsolate ladies of the Household, a grand-daughter of the Master had a wondrous dream of Him; He was speaking with His beloved sister, the Greatest Holy Leaf, in the very room where, in the early hours of the day, it was the custom of the ladies to assemble in His presence, chanting the morning prayers, and to take their morning tea. He turned to her and said: "Wherefore are ye all perturbed; why lament and be sorrowful? With you all I am well pleased. For a long time have I desired to join my Father, the Blessed Beauty. I was ever beseeching Him to take me to His Rosegarden above, and now that my prayer is granted, how happy, how joyous, how rested I am! Therefore grieve not." He then counselled them in many ways, exhorting them to follow at all times the commandments of Bahá'u'lláh.

Early on Monday morning the news of this

'Abdu'l-Bahá's Funeral

sudden calamity had spread over the city, causing an unprecedented stir and tumult, and filling all hearts with unutterable grief.

The next morning, Tuesday, the funeral took place, a funeral the like of which Haifa, nay Palestine itself, had surely never seen . . . so deep was the feeling that brought so many thousands of mourners together, representative of so many religions, races and tongues.

. . . On this day there was no cloud in the sky, nor any sound in all the town and surrounding country through which they went, save only the soft, slow, rhythmic chanting of Islám in the Call to Prayer, or the convulsed sobbing moan of those helpless ones, bewailing the loss of their one friend, who had protected them in all their difficulties and sorrows, whose generous bounty had saved them and their little ones from starvation through the terrible years of the "Great Woe".

"O God, my God!" the people wailed with one accord, "Our father has left us, our father has left us!"

O the wonder of that great throng! Peoples of every religion and race and colour, united in heart through the Manifestation of Servitude in the lifelong work of 'Abdu'l-Bahá!

As they slowly wended their way up Mount Carmel, the Vineyard of God, the casket appeared in the distance to be borne aloft by invisible hands, so high above the heads of the people was it carried. After two hours walking, they reached the garden of the Tomb of the

'Abdu'l-Bahá at Green Acre, 1912

Báb. Tenderly was the sacred coffin placed upon a plain table covered with a fair white linen cloth. As the vast concourse pressed round the Tabernacle of His body, waiting to be laid in its resting place, within the vault, next to that of the Báb, representatives of the various denominations, Moslems, Christians and Jews, all hearts being ablaze with fervent love of 'Abdu'l-Bahá, some on the impulse of the moment, others prepared, raised their voices in eulogy and regret, paying their last homage of farewell to their loved one. So united were they in their acclamation of him, as the wise educator and reconciler of the human race in this perplexed and sorrowful age, that there seemed to be nothing left for the Bahá'ís to say.

'Abdu'l-Bahá—Haifa

Taken in Haifa on 3 March 1921

THE passing of 'Abdu'l-Bahá, . . . marks the closing of the Heroic and Apostolic Age of this same Dispensation—that primitive period of our Faith the splendours of which can never be rivalled, much less be eclipsed, by the magnificence that must needs distinguish the future victories of Bahá'u'lláh's Revelation.

'Abdu'l-Bahá walking with Persian pilgrims on Mount Carmel

Significance of the Station of 'Abdu'l-Bahá

AN attempt I strongly feel should now be made to clarify our minds regarding the station occupied by 'Abdu'l-Bahá and the significance of His position in this holy Dispensation. It would indeed be difficult for us, who stand so close to such a tremendous figure and are drawn by the mysterious power of so magnetic a personality, to obtain a clear and exact understanding of the rôle and character of One Who, not only in the Dispensation of Bahá'u'-lláh but in the entire field of religious history, fulfils a unique function. Though moving in a sphere of His own and holding a rank radically different from that of the Author and the Forerunner of the Bahá'í Revelation, He, by virtue of the station ordained for Him through the Covenant of Bahá'u'lláh, forms together with Them what may be termed the Three Central Figures of a Faith that stands unapproached in the world's spiritual history. He towers, in conjunction with Them, above the destinies of this infant Faith of God from a level to which no individual or body ministering to its needs after Him, and for no less a period than a full thousand years, can ever hope to rise. To degrade His lofty rank by identifying His station with or by regarding it as roughly equivalent to, the position of those on whom the mantle of His

'Abdu'l-Bahá and Shoghi Effendi with group of pilgrims

Taken in front of No. 7 Haparsim Street

authority has fallen would be an act of impiety as grave as the no less heretical belief that inclines to exalt Him to a state of absolute equality with either the central Figure or Forerunner of our Faith. For wide as is the gulf that separates 'Abdu'l-Bahá from Him Who is the Source of an independent Revelation, it can never be regarded as commensurate with the greater distance that stands between Him Who is the Centre of the Covenant and His ministers who are to carry on His work, whatever be their name, their rank, their functions or their future achievements. Let those who have known 'Abdu'l-Bahá, who through their contact with His magnetic personality have come to cherish for Him so fervent an admiration, reflect, in the light of this statement, on the greatness of One Who is so far above Him in station.

That 'Abdu'l-Bahá is not a Manifestation of God, that, though the successor of His Father, He does not occupy a cognate station, that no one else except the Báb and Bahá'u'lláh can ever lay claim to such a station before the expiration of a full thousand years—are verities which lie embedded in the specific utterances of both the Founder of our Faith and the Interpreter of His teachings.

"*Whoso layeth claim to a Revelation direct from God,*" is the express warning uttered in the Kitáb-i-Aqdas, "*ere the expiration of a full thousand years, such a man is assuredly a lying impostor. We pray God that He may graciously assist him to retract and repudiate such claim. Should he repent, God will* no doubt forgive him. If, however, he persists in his error, God will assuredly send down one who will deal mercilessly with him. Terrible indeed is God in punishing." "Whosoever," He adds as a further emphasis, "*interpreteth this verse otherwise than its obvious meaning is deprived of the Spirit of God and of His mercy which encompasseth all created things.*" "*Should a man appear,*" is yet another conclusive statement, "*ere the lapse of a full thousand years—each year consisting of twelve months according to the Qur'án, and of nineteen months of nineteen days each, according to the Bayán—and if such a man reveal to your eyes all the signs of God, unhesitatingly reject him!*"

* * *

'Abdu'l-Bahá, Who incarnates an institution for which we can find no parallel whatsoever in any of the world's recognized religious systems, may be said to have closed the Age to which He Himself belonged and opened the one in which we are now labouring. His Will and Testament should thus be regarded as the perpetual, the indissoluble link which the mind of Him Who is the Mystery of God has conceived in order to ensure the continuity of the three ages that constitute the component parts of the Bahá'í Dispensation. The period in which the seed of the Faith had been slowly germinating is thus intertwined both with the one which must witness its efflorescence and the subsequent age in which that seed will have finally yielded its golden fruit.

'Abdu'l-Bahá with German officers in Haifa

'Abdu'l-Bahá and Shoghi Effendi at No. 7 Haparsim Street

Greatest Holy Leaf, circa 1890

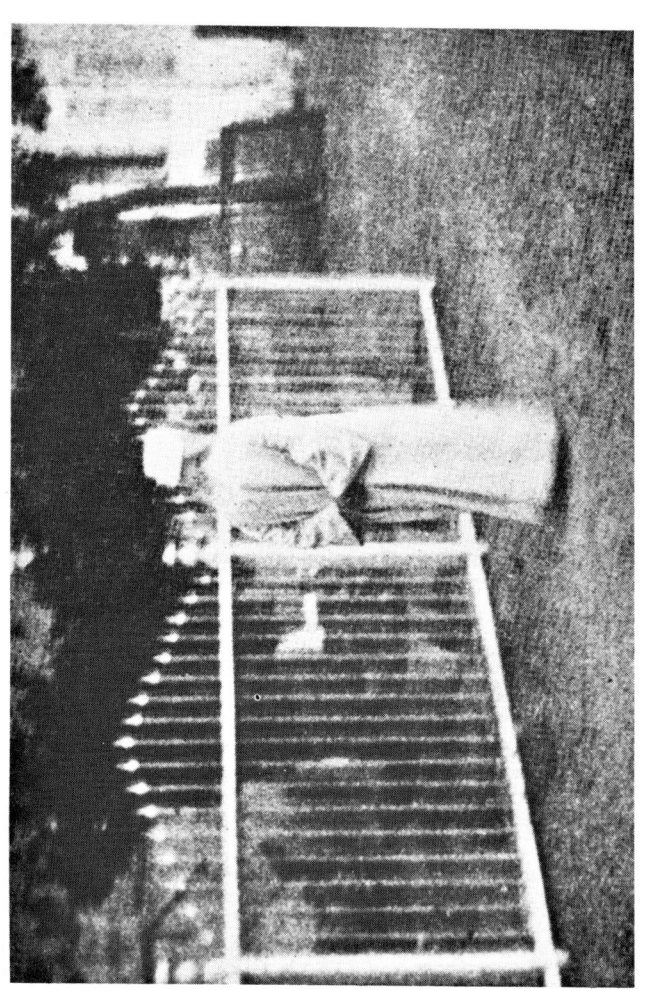

'Abdu'l-Bahá at Bahjí

Extracts from the Will and Testament of 'Abdu'l-Bahá

O ye that stand fast in the Covenant! When the hour cometh that this wronged and broken-winged bird will have taken its flight unto the Celestial concourse, when it will have hastened to the Realm of the Unseen and its mortal frame will have been either lost or hidden neath the dust, it is incumbent upon the Afnán, that are steadfast in the Covenant of God, and have branched from the Tree of Holiness; the Hands (pillars) of the Cause of God (the glory of the Lord rest upon them), and all the friends and loved ones, one and all to bestir themselves and arise with heart and soul and in one accord, to diffuse the sweet savours of God, to teach His Cause, and to promote His Faith. It behooveth them not to rest for a moment, neither to seek repose. They must disperse themselves in every land, pass by every clime, and travel throughout all regions. Bestirred, without rest, and steadfast to the end they must raise in every land the triumphal cry "O Thou the Glory of Glories!" (Yá Bahá'u'l-Abhá), must achieve renown in the world wherever they go, must burn brightly even as a candle in every meeting, and must kindle the flame of Divine love in every assembly; that the light of truth may rise resplendent in

the midmost heart of the world, that throughout the East and throughout the West a vast concourse may gather under the shadow of the Word of God, that the sweet savours of holiness may be diffused, that faces may shine radiantly, hearts be filled with the Divine spirit, and souls be made heavenly.

In these days, the most important of all things is the guidance of the nations and peoples of the world. Teaching the Cause is of utmost importance for it is the head corner-stone of the foundation itself. This wronged servant has spent his days and nights in promoting the Cause and urging the peoples to service. He rested not a moment, till the fame of the Cause of God was noised abroad in the world and the Celestial strains from the Abhá Kingdom roused the East and West. The beloved of God must also follow the same example. This is the secret of faithfulness, this is the requirement of servitude to the Threshold of Bahá!

The disciples of Christ forgot themselves and all earthly things, forsook all their cares and belongings, purged themselves of self and passion, and with absolute detachment scattered far and wide and engaged in calling the peoples of the world to the Divine Guidance, till at last they made the world another world, illumined the surface of the earth, and even to their last hour proved self-sacrificing in the pathway of that Beloved One of God. Finally in various lands they suffered glorious martyrdom. Let them that are men of action follow in their footsteps!

At No. 7 Haparsim Street

O my loving friends! After the passing away of this wronged one, it is incumbent upon the Aghsán (Branches), the Afnán (Twigs) of the Sacred Lote-Tree, the Hands (pillars) of the Cause of God, and the loved ones of the Abhá Beauty to turn unto Shoghi Effendi—the youthful branch branched from the Two hallowed and sacred Lote-trees and the fruit grown from the union of the Two offshoots of the Tree of Holiness —as he is the sign of God, the chosen branch, the guardian of the Cause of God, he unto whom all the Aghsán, the Afnán, the Hands of the Cause of God, and His loved ones must turn. He is the expounder of the words of God and after him will succeed the first born of his lineal descendants.

The sacred and youthful branch, the guardian of the Cause of God as well as the Universal House of Justice, to be universally elected and established, are both under the care and protection of the Abhá Beauty, under the shelter and unerring guidance of His Holiness, the Exalted One (may my life be offered up for them both). Whatsoever they decide is of God. Whoso obeyeth him not, neither obeyeth them, hath not obeyed God; whoso rebelleth against him and against them hath rebelled against God; whoso opposeth him hath opposed God; whoso contendeth with them hath contended with God; whoso disputeth with him hath disputeth with God; whoso denieth him hath denied God; whoso disbelieveth in him hath disbelieved in God; whoso deviateth, separateth himself, and turneth aside from him hath in truth deviated,

'Abdu'l-Bahá with child outside His house in Haifa

separated himself, and turned aside from God. May the wrath, the fierce indignation, the vengeance of God rest upon him! The mighty stronghold shall remain impregnable and safe through obedience to him who is the guardian of the Cause of God. It is incumbent upon the House of Justice, upon all the members of the Aghsán, the Afnán, the Hands of the Cause of God to show their obedience, submissiveness, and subordination unto the guardian of the Cause of God, to turn unto him and be lowly before him.

The Greatest Holy Leaf

AS far back as the concluding stages of the heroic age of the Cause, which witnessed the imprisonment of Bahá'u'lláh in the Síyáh-Chál of Ṭihrán, the Greatest Holy Leaf, then still in her infancy, was privileged to taste of the cup of woe which the first believers of that apostolic age had quaffed.

*   *   *

The stress and storm of that period made an abiding impression upon her mind, and she retained till the time of her death on her beauteous and angelic face evidences of its intense harships.

Not until, however, she had been confined in the company of Bahá'u'lláh within the walls of the prison-city of 'Akká did she display, in the plenitude of her power and in the full abundance of her love for Him, more gifts that single her out, next to 'Abdu'l-Bahá, among the members of the Holy Family, as the brightest embodiment of that love which is born of God and of that human sympathy which few mortals are capable of evincing.

Banishing from her mind and heart every earthly attachment, renouncing the very idea of matrimony, she, standing resolutely by the side of a Brother whom she was to aid and serve so

'Abdu'l-Bahá writing at No. 7 Haparsim Street

well, arose to dedicate her life to the service of her Father's glorious Cause. Whether in the management of the affairs of His Household in which she excelled, or in the social relationships which she so assiduously cultivated in order to shield both Bahá'u'lláh and 'Abdu'l-Bahá, whether in the unfailing attention she paid to the everyday needs of her Father, or in the traits of generosity, of affability and kindness, which she manifested, the Greatest Holy Leaf had by that time abundantly demonstrated her worthiness to rank as one of the noblest figures intimately associated with the lifelong work of Bahá'u'lláh.

* * *

And when, in pursuance of God's insrcutable Wisdom the ban on 'Abdu'l-Bahá's confinement was lifted and the Plan which He, in the darkest hours of His confinement, had conceived materialized, He, with unhesitating confidence, invested His trusted and honoured sister with the responsibility of attending to the multitudinous details arising out of His protracted absence from the Holy Land.

No sooner had 'Abdu'l-Bahá stepped upon the shores of the European and American continents than our beloved K͟hánum found herself wellnigh overwhelmed with thrilling messages, each betokening the irresistible advance of the Cause in a manner which, notwithstanding the vast range of her experience, seemed to her almost incredible. The years in which she basked in the sunshine of 'Abdu'l-Bahá's spiritual victories were, perhaps,

'Abdu'l-Bahá in Haifa

among the brightest and happiest of her life. Little did she dream when, as a little girl, she was running about, in the courtyard of her Father's house in Ṭihrán, in the company of Him Whose destiny was to be one day the chosen Centre of God's indestructible Covenant, that such a Brother would be capable of achieving, in realms so distant, and among races so utterly remote, so great and memorable a victory.

The enthusiasm and joy which swelled in her breast as she greeted 'Abdu'l-Bahá on His triumphant return from the West I will not venture to describe. She was astounded at the vitality of which He had, despite His unimaginable sufferings, proved Himself capable. She was lost in admiration at the magnitude of the forces which His utterances had released. She was filled with thankfulness to Bahá'u'lláh for having enabled her to witness the evidences of such brilliant victory for His Cause no less than for His Son.

*   *   *

The ascension of 'Abdu'l-Bahá, so tragic in its suddenness, was to her a terrific blow, from the effects of which she never completely recovered. To her He, whom she called "Aqá", had been a refuge in times of adversity. On Him she had been led to place her sole reliance. In Him she had found ample compensation for the bereavements she had suffered, the desertions she had witnessed, the ingratitude she had been shown by friends and kindred. No one could ever dream

Taken from the gate of No. 7 Haparsim Street

that a woman of her age, so frail in body, so sensitive of heart, so loaded with the cares of almost eighty years of incessant tribulation, could so long survive so shattering a blow. And yet history, no less than the annals of our immortal Faith, shall record for her a share in the advancement and consolidation of the world-wide community which the hand of 'Abdu'l-Bahá had helped to fashion, which no one among the remnants of His Family can rival.

* * *

It would take me too long to make even a brief allusion to those incidents of her life, each of which eloquently proclaims her as a daughter worthy to inherit that priceless heritage bequeathed to her by Bahá'u'lláh. A purity of life that reflected itself in even the minutest details of her daily occupations and activities; a tenderness of heart that obliterated every distinction of creed, class, and colour; a resignation and serenity that evoked to the mind the calm and heroic fortitude of the Báb; a natural fondness for flowers and children that was so characteristic of Bahá'u'lláh; an unaffected simplicity of manners; an extreme sociability which made her accessible to all; a generosity, a love, at once disinterested and undiscriminating, that reflected so clearly the attributes of 'Abdu'l-Bahá's character; a sweetness of temper; a cheerfulness that no amount of sorrow could becloud; a quiet and unassuming disposition that served to enhance a thousandfold the prestige of her exalted rank; a forgiving nature

'Abdu'l-Bahá

that instantly disarmed the most unyielding enemy—these rank among the outstanding attributes of a saintly life which history will acknowledge as having been endowed with a celestial potency that few of the heroes of the past possessed.

No wonder that in Tablets, which stand as eternal testimonies to the beauty of her character, Bahá'u'lláh and 'Abdu'l-Bahá have paid touching tributes to those things that testify to her exalted position among the members of their Family, that proclaim her as an example to their followers, and as an object worthy of the admiration of all mankind.

AS a further testimony to the majestic unfoldment and progressive consolidation of the stupendous undertaking launched by Bahá'u'lláh on that holy mountain, may be mentioned the selection of a portion of the school property situated in the precincts of the Shrine of the Báb as a permanent resting place for the Greatest Holy Leaf, the *"well-beloved"* sister of 'Abdu'l-Bahá, the *"Leaf that hath sprung"* from the *"Pre-existent Root"*, the *"fragrance* of Bahá'u'lláh's *"shining robe"*, elevated by Him to a *"station such as none other woman hath surpassed"*, and comparable in rank to those immortal heroines such as Sarah, 'Asíyih, the Virgin Mary, Fáṭimih and Ṭáhirih, each of whom has outshone every member of her sex in previous Dispensations.

Passages from Tablets revealed by Bahá'u'lláh

HE is the Eternal! This is My testimony for her who hath heard My voice and drawn nigh unto Me. Verily, she is a leaf that hath sprung from this Pre-existent Root. She hath revealed herself in My name and tasted of the sweet savours of My holy, My wondrous pleasure. At one time We gave her to drink from My honeyed Mouth, at another caused her to partake of My mighty, My luminous Kaw<u>th</u>ar. Upon her rest the glory of My name and the fragrance of My shining robe.

Let these exalted words be thy love-song on the tree of Bahá, O thou most holy and resplendent Leaf: 'God, besides Whom is none other God, the Lord of this world and the next!' Verily, We have elevated thee to the rank of one of the most distinguished among thy sex, and granted thee, in My court, a station such as none other woman hath surpassed. Thus have We preferred thee and raised thee above the rest, as a sign of grace from Him Who is the Lord of the throne on high and earth below. We have created thine eyes to behold the light of My countenance, thine ears to hearken unto the melody of My words, thy body to pay homage before My throne. Do thou render thanks unto God, thy Lord, the Lord of all the world.

How high is the testimony of the Sadratu'l-

'Abdu'l-Bahá entering His garden

Muntahá for its leaf; how exalted the witness of the Tree of Life unto its fruit! Through My remembrance of her a fragrance laden with the perfume of musk hath been diffused; well is it with him that hath inhaled it and exclaimed: 'All praise be to Thee, O God, my Lord the most glorious!' How sweet thy presence before Me; how sweet to gaze upon thy face to bestow upon thee My loving-kindness, to favour thee with My tender care, to make mention of thee in this, My Tablet—a Tablet which I have ordained as a token of My hidden and manifest grace unto thee.

Passages from Tablets revealed by 'Abdu'l-Bahá

O my well-beloved, deeply spiritual sister! Day and night thou livest in my memory. Whenever I remember thee my heart swelleth with sadness and my regret groweth more intense. Grieve not, for I am thy true, thy unfailing comforter. Let neither despondency nor despair becloud the serenity of thy life, or restrain thy freedom. These days shall pass away. We will, please God, in the 'Abhá Kingdom and beneath the sheltering shadow of the Blessed Beauty, forget all these our earthly cares and will find each one of these base calumnies amply compensated by His expressions of praise and favour. From the beginning of time sorrow and anxiety, regret and tribulation, have always been the lot of every loyal servant of God. Ponder this in thine heart and consider how very true it is. Wherefore, set thine heart on the tender mercies of the Ancient Beauty and be thou filled with abiding joy and intense gladness. . . .

Greatest Holy Leaf as a young woman

Greatest Holy Leaf

O thou my affectionate sister! In the day-time and in the night-season my thoughts ever turn to thee. Not for one moment do I cease to remember thee. My sorrow and regret concern not myself; they centre around thee. Whenever I recall thine afflictions, tears that I cannot repress rain down from mine eyes. . . .

EAR and deeply spiritual sister! At morn and eventide, with the utmost ardour and humility, I supplicate at the Divine Threshold, and offer this, my prayer:

"Grant, O Thou my God, the Compassionate, that that pure and blessed Leaf may be comforted by Thy sweet savours of holiness and sustained by the reviving breeze of Thy loving care and mercy. Reinforce her spirit with the signs of Thy Kingdom, and gladden her soul with the testimonies of Thy everlasting dominion. Comfort, O my God, her sorrowful heart with the remembrance of Thy face, initiate her into Thy hidden mysteries, and inspire her with the revealed splendours of Thy heavenly light. Manifold are her sorrows, and infinitely grievous her distress. Bestow continually upon her the favour of Thy sustaining grace, and with every fleeting breath, grant her the blessing of Thy bounty. Her hopes and expectations are centred in Thee; open Thou to her face the portals of Thy tender mercies and lead her into the ways of Thy wondrous benevolence. Thou art the Generous, the All-loving, the Sustainer, the All-bountiful."

Greatest Holy Leaf

Greatest Holy Leaf with Lady Blomfield, 22 May 1922

DEAR sister, beloved of my heart and soul! The news of thy safe arrival and pleasant stay in the land of Egypt has reached me and filled my heart with exceeding gladness. I am thankful to Bahá'u'lláh for the good health thou dost enjoy and for the happiness He hath imparted to the hearts of the loved ones in that land. Shouldst thou wish to know of the condition of this servant of the Threshold of the Abhá Beauty, praise be to Him for having enabled me to inhale the fragrance of His tender mercy and partake of the delights of His loving-kindness and blessings. I am being continually reinforced by the energizing rays of His grace, and feel upheld by the uninterrupted aid of the victorious hosts of His Kingdom. My physical health is also improving. God be praised that from every quarter I receive the glad-tidings of the growing ascendancy of the Cause of God, and can witness evidences of the increasing influence of its spread.

MY sister and beloved of my soul! I can never, never forget thee. However great the distance that separates us, we still feel as though we were seated under the same roof, in one and the same gathering, for are we not all under the shadow of the Tabernacle of God and beneath the canopy of His infinite grace and mercy?

Greatest Holy Leaf, 1931

Last photograph of Greatest Holy Leaf, taken by Effie Baker

O thou my loving, my deeply spiritual sister! I trust that by the grace and loving-kindness of the one true God thou art, and wilt be, kept safe and secure beneath the sheltering shadow of the Blessed Beauty. Night and day thy countenance appeareth before mine eyes, and in my mind are engraved the traits of thy character.

The Purest Branch

TO the galling weight of these tribulations was now added the bitter grief of a sudden tragedy—the premature loss of the noble, the pious Mírzá Mihdí, the Purest Branch, 'Abdu'l-Bahá's twenty-two-year-old brother, an amanuensis of Bahá'u'lláh and a companion of His exile from the days when, as a child, he was brought from Ṭihrán to Bag͟hdád to join His father after His return from Sulaymáníyyih. He was pacing the roof of the barracks in the twilight, one evening, wrapped in his customary devotions, when he fell through the unguarded skylight on to a wooden crate, standing on the floor beneath, which pierced his ribs, and caused, twenty-two hours later, his death, on the 23rd of Rabí'u'l-Avval 1287 A.H. (June 23, 1870). His dying supplication to a grieving Father was that his life might be accepted as a ransom for those who were prevented from attaining the presence of their Beloved.

In a highly significant prayer, revealed by Bahá'u'lláh in memory of His son—a prayer that exalts his death to the rank of those great acts of atonement associated with Abraham's intended sacrifice of His son, with the crucifixion of Jesus Christ and the martyrdom of the Imám Ḥusayn—we read the following: '*I have, O my Lord, offered up that which Thou hast given Me, that*

Thy servants may be quickened, and all that dwell on earth be united.' And, likewise, these prophetic words, addressed to His martyred son: '*Thou art the Trust of God and His Treasure in this Land. Erelong will God reveal through thee that which He hath desired.*'

After he had been washed in the presence of Bahá'u'lláh, he '*that was created of the light of Bahá,*' to whose '*meekness*' the Supreme Pen had testified, and of the '*mysteries*' of whose ascension that same Pen had made mention, was borne forth, escorted by the fortress guards, and laid to rest, beyond the city walls, in a spot adjacent to the shrine of Nabí Ṣáliḥ, from whence, seventy years later, his remains, simultaneously with those of his illustrious mother, were to be translated to the slopes of Mt. Carmel, in the pecincts of the grave of his sister, and under the shadow of the Báb's holy sepulchre.

'Abdu'l-Bahá with Purest Branch

Taken at Pilgrim House, 11 April 1921

'AT this very moment,' Bahá'u'lláh testifies, '*My son is being washed before My face after Our having sacrificed him in the Most Great Prison. Thereat have the dwellers of the Abhá Tabernacle wept with a great weeping, and such as have suffered imprisonment with this Youth in the path of God, the Lord of the promised Day, lamented. Under such conditions My Pen hath not been prevented from remembering its Lord, the Lord of all nations. It summoneth the people unto God, the Almighty, the All-Bountiful. This is the day whereon he that was created of the light of Bahá has suffered martyrdom, at a time when he lay imprisoned at the hands of his enemies.*'

'*Upon thee, O Branch of God!*' He solemnly and most touchingly, in that same Tablet, bestows upon him His benediction, '*be the remembrance of God and His praise, and the praise of all that dwell in the Realms of Immortality and of all the denizens of the Kingdom of Names. Happy art thou in that thou hast been faithful to the Covenent of God and His Testament, until Thou didst sacrifice thyself before the face of thy Lord, the Almighty, the Unconstrained. Thou, in truth, hast been wronged, and to this testifieth the Beauty of Him, the Self-Subsisting. Thou didst, in the first days of my life, bear that which hath caused all things to groan, and made every pillar to tremble. Happy is the one that remembereth thee, and draweth nigh, through thee, unto God, the Creator of the Morn.*'

'*Glorified art Thou, O Lord My God!*' He, in a prayer, astoundingly proclaims, '*Thou seest me in the hands of Mine enemies, and My son blood-stained before Thy face, O Thou in Whose hands is the kingdom* of all names, I have, O my Lord, offered up that which Thou hast given Me, that Thy servants may be quickened and all that dwell on earth be united.'

'*Blessed art thou*,' He, in another Tablet, affirms, '*and blessed he that turneth unto thee, and visiteth thy grave, and draweth nigh, through thee, unto God, the Lord of all that was and shall be . . . I testify that thou didst return in meekness unto thine abode. Great is thy blessedness and the blessedness of them that hold fast unto the hem of thy outspread robe . . . Thou art, verily, the trust of God and His treasure in this land. Ere long will God reveal through thee that which He hath desired. He, verily, is the Truth, the Knower of things unseen. When thou wast laid to rest in the earth, the earth itself trembled in its longing to meet thee. Thus hath it been decreed, and yet the people perceive not . . . Were We to recount the mysteries of thine ascension, they that are asleep would awaken, and all beings would be set ablaze with the fire of the remembrance of My Name, the Mighty, the Loving.*'

Navváb

CONCERNING the Most Exalted Leaf, the mother of 'Abdu'l-Bahá, Bahá'u'lláh has written: '*The first Spirit through which all spirits were revealed, and the first Light by which all lights shone forth, rest upon thee, O Most Exalted Leaf, thou who hast been mentioned in the Crimson Book! Thou art the one whom God created to arise and serve His own Self, and the Manifestation of His Cause, and the Dayspring of His Revelation, and the Dawning-Place of His signs, and the Source of His commandments: and Who so aided thee that thou didst turn with thy whole being unto Him, at a time when His servants and handmaidens had turned away from His face . . . Happy art thou, O my handmaiden, and My leaf, and the one mentioned in My Book, and inscribed by My Pen of Glory in My Scrolls and Tablets . . . Rejoice thou, at this moment, in the most exalted Station and the All-highest Paradise, and the Abhá Horizon, inasmuch as He Who is the Lord of Names hath remembered thee. We bear witness that thou didst attain unto all good, and that God hath so exalted thee, that all honour and glory circled around thee.*'

'*O Navváb!*' He thus, in another Tablet, addresses her, '*O Leaf that hath sprung from My Tree, and been My companion! My glory be upon thee, and My loving-kindness and My mercy that hath surpassed all beings. We announce unto thee that which will*

'Abdu'l-Bahá on way to Mosque, 27 October 1921

'Abdu'l-Bahá in Haifa garden

gladden thine eye, and assure thy soul, and rejoice thine heart. Verily, thy Lord is the Compassionate, the All-Bountiful. God hath been and will be pleased with thee, and hath singled thee out for His own Self, and chosen thee from among His hand-maidens to serve Him, and hath made thee the companion of His Person in the day-time and in the night-season.'

'Hear thou Me once again,' He reassures her, *'God is well-pleased with thee, as a token of His grace and a sign of His mercy. He hath made thee to be His companion in every one of His worlds and hath nourished thee with His meeting and presence, so long as His Name, and His Remembrance, and His Kingdom, and His Empire shall endure. Happy is the handmaid that hath mentioned thee, and sought thy good pleasure, and humbled herself before thee, and held fast unto the cord of thy love. Woe betide him that denieth thy exalted station, and things ordained for thee from God, the Lord of all names, and him that hath turned away from thee, and rejected thy station before God, the Lord of the mighty throne.'*

'O faithful ones!', Bahá'u'lláh specifically enjoins, *'Should ye visit the resting place of the Most Exalted Leaf, who hath ascended unto the Glorious Companion, stand ye and say: "Salutation and blessing and glory upon thee, O Holy Leaf that hath sprung from the Divine Lote-Tree! I bear witness that thou hast believed in God and in His signs, and answered His Call, and turned unto Him, and held fast unto His cord, and clung to the hem of His grace, and fled thy home in His path, and chosen to live as a stranger, out of love for His presence and in thy longing to serve Him. May God have mercy upon him that draweth nigh unto thee, and*

remembereth thee through the things which My Pen hath voiced in this, the most great station. We pray God that He may forgive us, and forgive them that have turned unto thee, and grant their desires, and bestow upon them, through His wondrous grace, whatever be their wish. He, verily, is the Bountiful, the Generous. Praise be to God, He Who is the Desire of all worlds, and the Beloved of all who recognize Him.'

And finally, 'Abdu'l-Bahá Himself in one of His remarkably significant Tablets, has borne witness not only to the exalted station of one whose '*seed shall inherit the Gentiles*', whose Husband is the Lord of Hosts, but also the sufferings endured by her who was His beloved mother. 'As to thy question concerning the 54th chapter of Isaiah,' He writes, '*This chapter refers to the Most Exalted Leaf, the mother of 'Abdu'l-Bahá. As a proof of this it is said: "For more are the children of the desolate, than the children of the married wife." Reflect upon this statement and then upon the following: "And thy seed shall inherit the Gentiles, and make the desolate cities to be inhabited." And truly the humiliation and reproach which she suffered in the path of God is a fact which no one can refute. For the calamities and afflictions mentioned in the whole chapter are such afflictions which she suffered in the path of God, all of which she endured with patience and thanked God therefor and praised Him, because He had enabled her to endure afflictions for the sake of Bahá. During all this time, the men and women (Covenant-breakers) persecuted her in an incomparable manner, while she was patient, God-fearing, calm, humble, and contented through the favour of her Lord and by the bounty of her Creator.*'

The Tablet of Visitation

Whoso reciteth this prayer with lowliness and fervour will bring gladness and joy to the heart of this servant; it will be even as meeting Him face to face.

HE is the All Glorious! O God, my God! Lowly and tearful, I raise my suppliant hands to Thee and cover my face in the dust of that Threshold of Thine, exalted above the knowledge of the learned, and the praise of all that glorify Thee. Graciously look upon Thy servant, humble and lowly at Thy door, with the glances of the eye of Thy mercy, and immerse him in the Ocean of Thine eternal grace.

Lord! He is a poor and lowly servant of Thine, enthralled and imploring Thee, captive in Thy hand, praying fervently to Thee, trusting in Thee, in tears before Thy face, calling to Thee and beseeching Thee, saying:

O Lord, my God! Give me Thy grace to serve Thy loved ones, strengthen me in my servitude to Thee, illumine my brow with the light of adoration in Thy court of holiness, and of prayer to Thy Kingdom of grandeur. Help me to be selfless at the heavenly entrance of Thy gate, and aid me to be detached from all things within Thy holy precincts. Lord! Give me to

drink from the chalice of selflessness; with its robe clothe me, and in its ocean immerse me. Make me as dust in the pathway of Thy loved ones, and grant that I may offer up my soul for the earth ennobled by the footsteps of Thy chosen ones in Thy path, O Lord of Glory in the Highest.

With this prayer doth Thy servant call Thee, at dawn-tide, and in the night season. Fulfil his heart's desire, O Lord! Illumine his heart, gladden his bosom, kindle his light, that he may serve Thy Cause and Thy servants.

Thou art the Bestower, the Pitiful, the Most Bountiful, the Gracious, the Merciful, the Compassionate!

—*'Abdu'l-Bahá*

"I am the lamp and the love of God is my light."

—*'Abdu'l-Bahá*

Abbreviations

G.P.B.	God Passes By
D.O.B.	Dispensation of Bahá'u'lláh
T.O.B.	Tablets of Bahá'u'lláh
S.O.W.	Star of the West
B.O.F.	Bahá'í World Faith
P.O.U.P.	Promulgation of Universal Peace
B.R.	Bahá'í Revelation
W.O.B.	World Order of Bahá'u'lláh
G.F.T.&T.	Guidance for Today & Tomorrow
B.H.P.	Bahá'í Holy Places

References

Page(s)
- 8   G.P.B., p. 309
- 17   D.O.B 1947, pp. 44–5
- 18   T.O.B. 1978, pp. 221–2
- 21   D.O.B. (Su'riy-i-Ghusn), p. 45
- 22   D.O.B., pp. 45–6
- 25   D.O.B., p. 44
- 26   S.O.W. Vol. VIII, p. 186
- 29   B.W.F. 1971, pp. 358–9
- 30   P.O.U.P. 1943, p. 317
- 35   B.R. quote from European Teaching Manual 1948
- 36   B.R.
- 41   G.P.B., p. 239
- 43   S.O.W. Vol. X, p. 227
- 46   P.O.U.P. 1943, pp. 240–1
- 49   W.O.B., p. 135
- 51   W.O.B., pp. 135–6

References

52	W.O.B., p. 135
55	W.O.B., p. 136
56	W.O.B., p. 136
61–68	G.P.B., pp. 240–2
72	G.P.B., p. 243
74	G.P.B., p. 245
77	G.P.B., p. 245
79	G.P.B., p. 264
80–93	G.P.B., pp. 267–72
97–107	G.P.B., pp. 273–5
110–15	G.P.B., pp. 275–6
115–27	G.P.B., pp. 279–83
131	G.P.B., p. 283
135–48	G.P.B., pp. 290–2
153–69	G.P.B., pp. 292–4
165–71	P.O.U.P.
174–9	P.O.U.P.
184–90	P.O.U.P.
192–8	P.O.U.P.
200–6	T.O.D.P.
208–16	T.O.D.P.
219–31	G.P.B., pp. 303–7
233	G.P.B., p. 309
234–9	G.P.B., pp. 309–10
243–59	The Passing of 'Abdu'l-Bahá
264	D.O.B., p. 53
266–70	D.O.B., pp. 41–54
275–81	The Will and Testament of 'Abdu'l-Bahá
282	First para. G.P.B., p. 108
282–90	G.F.T.&T., pp. 59–69
292	G.P.B., p. 347
293–308	B.H.P., pp. 65–9
309–10	G.P.B., pp. 188–9
315–16	G.F.T.&T., pp. 72–4
317–21	G.F.T.&T., pp. 74–6

Acknowledgements

Colour photograph from original painting by Mr. R. Samimí

All other photographs courtesy of the Audio Visual Department of the Universal House of Justice